T0351820

Collaborative Crisis Management

Collaborative Crisis Management

PREPARE, EXECUTE,
RECOVER, REPEAT

Thomas A. Cole and Paul Verbinnen

The University of Chicago Press CHICAGO AND LONDON

The University of Chicago Press, Chicago 60637
The University of Chicago Press, Ltd., London
© 2022 by Thomas A. Cole and Paul Verbinnen
Published 2022
Printed in the United States of America

31 30 29 28 27 26 25 24 23 22   1 2 3 4 5

ISBN-13: 978-0-226-82135-1 (cloth)
ISBN-13: 978-0-226-82137-5 (paper)
ISBN-13: 978-0-226-82136-8 (e-book)
DOI: https://doi.org/10.7208/chicago/9780226821368.001.0001

Library of Congress Cataloging-in-Publication Data

Names: Cole, Thomas A. (Lawyer), author. | Verbinnen, Paul, author.
Title: Collaborative crisis management : prepare, execute, recover, repeat /
Thomas A. Cole and Paul Verbinnen.
Description: Chicago : University of Chicago Press, 2022. |
Includes bibliographical references and index.
Identifiers: LCCN 2022000535 | ISBN 9780226821351 (cloth) |
ISBN 9780226821375 (paperback) | ISBN 9780226821368 (e-book)
Subjects: LCSH: Crisis management.
Classification: LCC HD49.C643 2022 | DDC 658.4/056—dc23/eng/20220119
LC record available at https://lccn.loc.gov/2022000535

♾ This paper meets the requirements of ANSI/NISO Z39.48-1992
(Permanence of Paper).

Contents

Introduction

This is a book about corporate crisis management. We focus on the US public company, because crisis management in that business context is, arguably, the most difficult and complex. It is also what we know best. In writing this book, we draw upon our collective nearly three-quarters of a century of experience in advising managements and boards of public companies in crisis.

There are many books about crisis management. This may be the only one co-authored by a lawyer and a communication consultant. While you may be able to tell which one of us "had the pen" on which chapters, we have collaborated fully on all content.

This book is also different from the others in the following ways:

- Most other books are narrowly focused on communications during the pendency of a crisis, often with a particular focus on shareholders. We believe a broader focus is required for successful crisis management.
- Certainly communications is a critical element of effective crisis management, and our chapter about communications is the longest in the book. (We also include an appendix in which we summarize the key recommendations about communications from prior literature and provide an extensive bibliography.) Nevertheless, as you can tell from the title and table of contents, we think that anyone in a position of leading a crisis management team needs to adopt a broader perspective and fully embrace the need for a multidisciplinary approach. Despite the fact that the various disciplines will not always align in their recommendations, a leader must insist on full collaboration, even under stressful conditions.
- Clearly actions taken during the pendency of a crisis deserve intense focus. Nevertheless, as you can tell from the subtitle of the book, we

believe that effective crisis management involves robust pre-crisis preparedness and thoughtful post-crisis introspection.

- We are also deeply attuned to the fiduciary duties that directors and officers owe to the shareholders. Nevertheless, in an age of emphasis on all stakeholders (but also to optimize outcomes for the shareholders), we believe that both the leader of a crisis management team and the board of directors will best serve the company's interests by adopting a perspective broad enough to consider the impact of the crisis, and how it is managed, on all of the company's constituencies—especially the employees.
- We emphasize the decision-making elements of crisis management— how to get the best inputs; where within the organization the decisions should be made; the need to be flexible and, on occasion, reverse course from prior decisions.
- We discuss managing crises that simultaneously affect multiple businesses in a single industry or that spill over from one company to another. While misery loves company, having that company can complicate the task.
- Finally, we are not presenting a handful of in-depth case studies, as is typical in many crisis management books. We are eschewing the case study approach for a variety of reasons. First and foremost, we have learned from experience that each crisis is sui generis. Put another way, if you've seen one crisis, you've seen one crisis! So, to our minds, a detailed description of only four or six crises doesn't capture all of the critical elements of crisis management. And, because some of the crisis management case studies we could best present in detail are those where we were professionally involved, we have ongoing obligations of confidentiality and can't talk about them. Our approach is to provide the reader with a mostly anonymous amalgam of lessons learned across all disciplines, from both crises where we had a front-row seat and those that we have observed from afar. That said, we do reference a number of crises by name, based upon publicly available information. The reader will see that most of those instances involve crises that could have been handled better. While it might be interesting to provide some positive examples, to use a medical analogy, we believe that more can be learned from "pathology" than from "wellness exams." Moreover, the crises that might fall into that latter category typically have very little information available publicly. This is because, in some ways, a really well-handled crisis is like the proverbial tree falling in the forest with no one around (other than insiders) to hear. Supplementing our own observations, at the end of Chapter 12 we report on some

lessons shared with us by CEOs and others who were intimately engaged in a variety of crisis situations. From all of that, we have tried to provide a useful discussion of all of the aspects of effective crisis management.

Independent of literature on crisis management, there is a field of sociological research devoted to disaster studies,[1] and there are many practical works on disaster management. While that subject presents some interesting analogies, the literature in that area is, obviously, focused on macro (not micro) events and often management by leaders in the public sector. Of course, a disaster can also result in a company-specific crisis.

We are not aspiring to write a "how-to" book—because, again, each crisis is unique. Rather, we think it is more useful to focus on what questions to ask in order to gather the best available information to inform decision-making and to help focus on the many different kinds of decisions that need to be made, often quickly and in real time.

We have organized this book in the four, essentially chronological parts foreshadowed in the subtitle. As already mentioned, in many ways the best approach to ensure success in managing a crisis is robust pre-crisis preparation. So, Part I is PREPARE. When the crisis hits, it is time to EXECUTE; hence, the title of Part II. When the dust has settled, it is time to RECOVER and, finally, be even better prepared to REPEAT if and when faced with the next crisis. Those are the subjects of Parts III and IV, respectively.

As noted above, this book focuses on crises at US public companies. However, we think that managements and boards of other types of organizations—private companies in all industries, as well as universities and other not-for-profits—will find it useful. Special considerations for leaders of those kinds of organizations will be covered in Part V.

We hope, too, that professionals who advise organizations in crisis and journalists who write about organizations in crisis will also find this book to be useful. Another audience is business, law, and journalism school professors who instruct future generations of managements, directors, lawyers, communications professionals, and other types of consultants.

From the publication date of this book, it should be apparent that we began writing it just before the outbreak of the COVID-19 Pandemic. (As more than one friend has stated to each of us over the past months, "you picked a helluva time to write about crises!") That historic event represents both a public health and an economic crisis. The Pandemic has required intense management by leaders in both the public and private sectors. In Part VI we offer some preliminary thoughts—based upon personal observation and public reporting through late 2021—about how some of the key elements we identify as being required for effective crisis management were either present or absent in the responses of public company leaders. We readily acknowledge that in 2020, and continuing into 2022, there were other crises—social, environmental, and political. The corporate response to those crises—including whether or not to speak out, especially on social or political issues—is important, but beyond the scope of this book.[2]

Finally, Part VII is a collection of most of the key questions that should be asked by corporate CEOs and board members, *early and often*—before, during, and after a crisis.

We hope that you, the reader, will find this book useful for dealing with crises. To be most useful, the entire book (or at least Part I) should be read *before* a crisis occurs. While we hope you will not have to manage a crisis, it would be an unusual organization that has a crisis-free existence. To paraphrase a popular bumper sticker, "crisis happens."

· I ·

Prepare

1

What Are the Common Themes? General Understandings Critical for Preparedness

While every crisis is different, a starting point for being prepared to deal with a crisis—even before undertaking concrete steps to prepare—is to understand, in general terms, the categories and commonalities of corporate crises and the current environment in which crises must be handled.

For an event or situation to deserve the label "crisis," it should be an existential threat, have a realistic risk that it could evolve into that kind of threat or, at least, have the potential to cause severe and lasting financial or reputational damage. Sometimes, it is hard to tell at the outset whether a bad event or situation is, or has the potential to mature into, a crisis. Many people will hesitate to express a view along those lines, lest they be labeled "Chicken Littles." But it is better to calmly anticipate that potential than to, Pollyannaishly, be caught flatfooted.

As we see it, there are four broad categories of crises, each of which can pose different degrees of difficulty of management:

- Category #1—Internally generated and core to the business. Examples of crises in this category are those related to defective products (e.g., Takata airbags), to fraudulent business practices (e.g., Wells Fargo and Volkswagen), to accidents at a principal facility (e.g., BP's Deepwater Horizon), to excessive financial risk (e.g., Credit Suisse/Archegos), or to issues arising following major acquisitions (e.g., Bayer/Monsanto).
- Category #2—Internally generated, but not resulting from activities that are pursued as part of a company's operation or strategy of the business. The most prominent (and regrettable) recent examples—dozens involving CEOs—are captured in the phrase #MeToo. Another example involves allegedly inappropriate surveillance of company executives (e.g., Credit Suisse).
- Category #3—Externally generated, targeting specific aspects of core business operations. The most prominent recent examples

are cyberattacks (many involving ransomware, like the Colonial Pipeline event) and mass shootings at a facility (tragically, too many to call out). Historically, the Tylenol tampering and murders (described in Appendix A) would fall into this category.

- Category #4—A disaster that broadly impacts virtually all aspects of a company's business. Certainly, the company-specific crises that resulted from the COVID-19 Pandemic and the attacks of 9/11 fall into this category.

Because we will be referencing this taxonomy of crises throughout the text (and especially in our discussion of executing crisis management), we have included a simplified chart showing these categories at the beginning of Part II.

While all the crises in each of these categories present management challenges and potentially an existential threat, corporations addressing those in Categories #3 and #4 are more likely to be viewed as victims. In Category #3, this will almost certainly be the case unless and until others conclude that those external events were predictable and the victims are faulted for a lack of preparation. (Examples of victims-at-fault are the Federal Trade Commission's fines of companies that were the victims of cyberattacks for "failure to take reasonable steps to secure [their] networks.") That means that crises in Categories #1 and #2 will more likely be labeled "scandals" and represent a greater degree of difficulty to address from an HR and reputational standpoint. Moreover, crises in Category #1 may pose a greater risk of financial exposure, adverse regulatory action, and corporate criminal liability than those in the other categories.

To be managed well, a crisis must be addressed by multidisciplinary teams, although the exact components may vary to some degree by the type and intensity of the situation. Operating management will certainly be appropriate team members in Categories #1 and #4. Members of management involved in finance, human resources, communications, and legal affairs will likely be involved in all categories. External counterparts with experience in crisis management can provide important supplemental support for those members of management. Because the different disciplines will bring different perspectives and opinions to a crisis, the teams will require a leader (or leaders) with the judgment and authority to mediate and reconcile the different approaches. All of this is discussed in more detail in Chapter 4.

Another general element of preparedness is to understand that crises go through fairly predictable life cycles:

- There is the early, "hair on fire" phase.

- Then, there is a more protracted period in which facts evolve, issues directly related to the crisis cascade, and second-order issues can develop. Among the potential second-order issues are securities and fiduciary duty litigation, attacks by shareholder activists, and loss of key personnel and funding support. This is also when "finger-pointing," "blame game," and accountability issues arise, often causing unique challenges for the organization.
- Eventually, there is a denouement, when the recovery phase described in Part III takes place. During this phase, the organization will be recovering organizationally, financially, and reputationally from the crisis and from second-order issues while also trying to understand the root cause of the crisis, especially one in Category #1.
- In the post-crisis period, the company should be assessing how well—or not—the crisis was managed, as discussed in Part IV.

In some ways, the most important advance understanding to have relates to the environment in which you are operating and managing the crisis. While the management of the 1982 Tylenol crisis by Johnson & Johnson deserved to be lauded as "a model for effective crisis management"[1] and should be studied,[2] the current environment is obviously vastly different than what J&J contended with nearly 40 years ago. Thus, the Tylenol example is only a starting point.

This is the current environment:

There are now requirements for intense board of director involvement in crises in the name of good corporate governance (which was only a nascent consideration in the early 1980s). Today, shareholders and the courts have very high expectations around board oversight of compliance and risk. CEOs should involve boards in robust risk management and, when a risk matures into an actual crisis, be prepared to provide frequent updates to the directors and anticipate board involvement in critical decisions. For their part, boards should insist on robust pre-crisis risk management and, on occasion, go beyond an oversight role in crisis management. They should also as a matter of course have a deep understanding of how the corporation's key stakeholders, including shareholders and regulators, perceive the company.

When a corporation finds itself in crisis, there are frequent calls for the termination of (or financial consequences to) a CEO or a change in the board, either for "allowing" the crisis to occur or for how the crisis is being handled. These calls can come from shareholder activists, politicians, regulators or, relating to the CEO, from his or her own directors. In a regulated industry, a CEO might not just be fired; a regulator could impose a lifetime ban.[3] When a corporation is subject to criminal exposure because of the facts underlying the crisis, there is now (at least theoretically) greater exposure of individual members of management.[4] And there is certainly a significant likelihood in today's world that a CEO will be dragged before a Congressional committee. His or her testimony would play out in a political environment that, to some degree, reflects an anti-corporate bias, hostility toward CEOs because of their high levels of compensation, and strongly held views (even of some CEOs) about flaws in the overall capitalist economic system. Anticipate the "profits over people" refrain. Finally, it is not without precedent that a CEO will simply quit rather than preside over managing the crisis.[5] (More on that in Chapter 4.)

Litigation risk is now greatly increased by emails and other digital documents that can be created without sufficient care in the "hair on fire" stage of the crisis, or even before any crisis, but that will never go away.

Increasingly, crises can affect entire industries. For example, the opioid epidemic yielded crises for multiple companies in each of the manufacturing, distribution, and retail segments. (Those crises, of course, pale in comparison to what individuals, families, and communities have had to deal with.) Plaintiff lawyers in league with activists have also become adept at targeting whole industries engaged in all manner of activities, from pesticides, electronic cigarettes, guns, oil and gas, and video games to medical products and more.

Because, of course, the corporations in an affected industry must generally respond individually, their responses inevitably will be viewed in the context of what the others are doing. Does the timing and/or size of the booking of an accounting reserve by one company impact the thinking of another (or of the Securities and Exchange Commission [SEC] or the outside auditors)? Does the speed of one company's product recall make the others look slow or, worse, unconcerned or casual? Does a decision by one company to plead guilty to criminal charges or accept a deferred prosecution agreement turn up the heat on others? Does a generous act of redemption (see Chapter 11) by one company make another look cheap?

Crises can also spill over from individual companies or industries to impact customers and suppliers, potentially to the point of plunging them into an equally challenging crisis. The auto manufacturers that were purchasers of Takata airbags were clearly impacted by that company's crisis. This crisis cost auto manufacturers hundreds of millions of dollars. Those companies that supplied components of the 737 MAX were hurt very badly, as were Boeing's airline customers. There is also the potential for a crisis at a company to draw in professional services firms. This has always been a risk for public accounting firms when an audit client has a crisis-level issue with its financial statements, but it can happen to other types of firms as well.

Turning again to the opioid epidemic for an example, the investigation of Purdue Pharma unearthed documents that led to a crisis at the company's consultants, McKinsey. Within days following the news stories about those documents, the global managing partner of McKinsey published a statement on its website: ". . . any suggestion that our work sought to increase overdoses or misuse and worsen public health is wrong. That said, we recognize that we have a responsibility to take into account the broader context and implications of the work we do. Our work for Purdue fell short of that standard."[6] A short time later, McKinsey agreed to a $573 million settlement with 47 states and the District of Columbia. After that, the senior partner was voted out of office, reportedly because, in response to the Purdue situation, he had been working to impose stricter risk management processes relating to client intake.[7]

As a result of this spillover potential, leaders of companies and of professional services firms should treat news of a crisis at a customer, supplier, or client as a possible "early warning" of a potential crisis of their own.

Perhaps the most challenging element of the current environment for crisis management is in the communications arena. The global news cycle is now measured in seconds and minutes, driven significantly by social media and cable/satellite/streaming news outlets. Electronic media has been justly accused of having a predilection for "gotcha" sound bites and aggressive editing of interviews. And there are arguably lower journalistic standards than in the past, at least at some outlets. Those who post on social media often have no standards beyond trying to attract "clicks and eyeballs," and only recently have platforms (e.g., Facebook, Twitter) begun to try to address "misinformation," a highly fraught and controversial effort in itself in today's polarized world. Rumor and innuendo can quickly metastasize in the minds of crucial audiences. The net effect can frequently pressure crisis management teams into making judgments on the fly and to issue communications that have not been given the attention that they deserve.

Another impact of the internet is how easy it makes research. So, in the current environment, news about a current crisis will often include an encyclopedic rehash of news about any previous crisis at the company—no matter how ancient or even unrelated. Communicators on behalf of a company will need to be prepared to answer, or deflect, questions about history that may predate their time with the company. And those questions may come with a hostile tone—"haven't you learned?"

Informed by these general understandings, it is easy to see that taking concrete steps to prepare for crisis scenarios, long before an actual crisis occurs, is a worthwhile exercise. And failing to do so creates even more risk for a company or other type of organization.

2

How Do We Prepare? Concrete Elements of Preparation

To be prepared to manage crises in the current environment, public corporations should engage in four principal categories of activity—traditional risk management; anticipatory disclosure; reputation management; and planning for shareholder activism.

The activities in the first two categories of preparation start with considering the threshold question "What kinds of crises should we be preparing for?" While the famous quote from Donald Rumsfeld about known knowns, known unknowns, and unknown unknowns was initially subject to some degree of head-scratching, over time the legitimacy of his categorizations has received considerable acceptance.[1] His categories echo another quote about measurable and unmeasurable uncertainty.[2] Finally, there is the notion of "black swan" events.[3] These concepts are worth pausing over from the standpoint of risk management and anticipatory disclosure. An obvious starting point for identifying the kinds of crises to prepare for is to think about the company's history, as well as being attuned to the kinds of crises that have befallen the peer group.

Essentially, you need to do the best you can to prepare for crises that are of a reasonably predictable type and are reasonably probable of coming to pass. Then you need to hope that your preparation will serve the corporation well when the unknown and/or unlikely events occur.

There are general categories of risk that apply to most companies (and other organizations):

- *Strategic Risk.* This kind of risk will often result from a disruptive technology or business practice being introduced by the competition. Or it could result from a failed effort to execute a new strategy.
- *Financial Risk.* This often manifests as a lack of liquidity, which can be the result of a variety of factors and/or be a byproduct of the other types of risk. For a financial institution, this risk can be the

result of excessive credit exposure to a single market sector or, even, a single customer or counterparty.

- *Casualty Risk.* This can result from fire, flood, accidents, product failures, or other forms of tort liability. Casualty risk can also result from mass shootings and other forms of criminal behavior.

- *Compliance Risk.* This can result from failures to comply with applicable laws or regulations, either intentionally on the part of a company or due to a rogue employee who violates company policy. For a public company, a failure to comply with laws and regulations pertaining to public disclosure can carry significant risk for both the company and, on occasion, individual directors and officers. And regulators and investors have recently given increased attention to the quality of disclosures about the subject known by the acronym "ESG" (environmental, social, and governance).

- *Cyber Risk.* This can be the result of an attack by competitors, criminals, state actors, or disgruntled current or former employees. The goal of the attack could be simple disruption, theft of information, or ransom. For a public company, cyber risk can include a failure to provide investors with adequate disclosures about vulnerabilities. For any company, cyber risk can include a failure to comply with regulatory and/or contractual obligations to notify others (such as customers) that there has been an attack.

- *Political Risk.* This might involve the expropriation of a facility operating in a foreign country. But even for purely "domestic" companies, there can be political risk associated with a trade war or other action that cuts off, or increases the cost of, critical supplies and component parts. More recently, political risk could be caused by a corporation speaking out or taking action on a politically or socially sensitive subject that leads to a consumer boycott or other retaliation by, or encouraged by, governments or politicians.

While most companies have to deal with these categories of risk, they combine in different ways for specific companies. Thus, one step for preparedness is to have a sense of the risk profile of the company. While companies in all industries have the potential for being plunged into crisis, some industries are more vulnerable than others. If nothing else, having a reasonable understanding of the company's risk profile and that of its industry will be relevant to a cost-benefit analysis on how much management and board time and company expense to devote to risk assessment and preparatory actions.

For example, consider the public utility industry. John Rowe, who was CEO of multiple public utilities for more than 25 years in total and is a past chair of both the Nuclear Energy Institute and the Edison Electric Institute, offered this wise perspective—"Utilities are a crisis-plagued industry because they serve everyone, they deal with dangerous hardware, they deal with politics all the time, they have large environmental impacts, and people die doing the work." Sometimes the risk profile of a company will be associated less with what industry it is in and more about where the company is in its life cycle and/or whether it is undergoing a major change in strategy. A period of rapid growth or one in which the company is changing how or where it operates can raise its risk profile.

Traditional Risk Management. The relationship between risk and crisis can be analogized to something taught in high school physics. A rock sitting on a cliff represents potential energy (a risk); when the rock plummets toward the house below, that is kinetic energy (causing crisis). If you live in the house, you would be wise to engage in risk management in order to prevent the fall of the rock or, at least, to mitigate the impact when it does fall. So, risk management is about both prevention and mitigation.

In the old days, if you asked to meet a company's risk manager, you were often introduced to the person who oversaw its **insurance** programs. Insurance certainly remains an important element of risk management, but from the standpoint of the insured, it principally focuses on mitigation. Of course, there can be a preventative element to an insurance program, to the extent that an insurer mandates certain behavior designed to prevent claims from being made. And the categories of insurance that can be purchased expand along with the proliferation of new types of risk. As but one example, consider cyber-insurance. But be sure to understand the exclusions written into any type of policy. Be sure, also, to understand the claims-paying ratings and financial stability of the insurance companies. Finally, future coverage availability and terms can be impacted by crises at peer companies or institutions.

Thoughtful modern risk management has many elements beyond insurance. There is corporate culture—a subject of such significance that it warrants its own chapter (Chapter 3). Other elements are quality control and assurance; corporate structure; capital structure; management structure and staffing; compensation design; war game exercises; information technology; and whistleblower hotlines.

For both manufacturers of goods and providers of services, **quality control and assurance** is part of risk management. Like insurance, this is a traditional element of risk management. A modern approach may require going beyond traditional, or at least static, sampling techniques. A financial institution that adopts an initiative to push its own people for sales may need to upgrade its supervision of the marketing and sales functions to assure that employees are not engaging in fraud. If a manufacturer subcontracts the production of its products and begins to aggressively squeeze pricing from its subcontractors, it may be appropriate to step up inspections both in factories and of finished goods (consider auto and aircraft manufacturers). Otherwise, efforts of subcontractors to preserve margins by substituting inferior raw materials or taking other shortcuts is a real possibility, which (in turn) can put customer well-being and company finances and reputation at risk.

John Rowe (quoted earlier) has observed generally that "crises tend to come from chronic problems not solved." Certainly, leaders of a company with chronic quality problems—no matter how seemingly minor, individually—that are not adequately addressed should be concerned that one day those problems could aggregate or worsen and result in a full-blown crisis. While the "broken windows theory" of urban policing (i.e., even minor transgressions should be addressed) has its issues, there may be something to be said for applying that theory in corporate risk management when it comes to quality control and assurance.

Corporate structure can be a risk mitigant. If a company has multiple lines of business and those lines present very different risk profiles, the business units that are the most risky might be best placed in subsidiaries and those subsidiaries placed at the bottom of the corporate organization chart. With that arrangement, if the risky unit were to fail, it may be possible to keep the assets of the other units out of the hands of creditors in a bankruptcy. In addition, internal financing relationships might be organized to prevent a failure of the risky business from dragging down the other businesses. For example, if possible, keep the less risky business units from being creditors of their risky affiliates or from being guarantors of their affiliates' external funding. Finally, if a risky business is in a corporate subsidiary or other form of limited liability enterprise, efforts should be made to prevent "veil piercing" by honoring legal formalities and other steps. "Veil piercing" is what happens when a judge is convinced to ignore the separateness of an entity (like a subsidiary) and subject its owner(s) (like a corporate parent) to that entity's liabilities.[4]

Another element of corporate structure is also relevant to risk management. Gillian Tett, a social anthropologist turned journalist, has argued persuasively that the presence of "silos" can create substantial risk for any type of organization.[5] Silos can be part of a formal structure that creates specialized departments. Even more of a culprit is a corporate culture that encourages (or doesn't discourage) "turf." Similarly, risk can be created by a leader who fails to bring together and listen to multidisciplinary teams or who engages in hub-and-spokes communications (with the leader being, of course, the hub). As a very simple example in the realm of communications, consider the many companies that fail to coordinate their investor relations, corporate communications, and SEC disclosure teams—even during a time of crisis.

Companies should consider another element of their financing and **capital structure** when thinking about risk management—namely, leverage. While institutional shareholders often criticize "inefficient" balance sheets and shareholder activists demand large share buybacks often funded by borrowings, when leverage is excessive (or events cause it to be excessive) it can lead to crisis. Thus, a comprehensive risk management program might include "stress testing." While this exercise is best known in the context of financial institutions, all kinds of companies may benefit. Companies should understand how their liquidity and cash flows might be affected by swings in expenses (interest rates, currency exchange rates, commodity prices) or events that cause a sudden and unexpected drop in revenues (a crisis at a customer or in any component of the supply chain) or even changes in their stock price or credit ratings. This exercise may lead to the conclusion that it would be prudent to engage in hedging transactions and/or to line up backup/excess liquidity lines as forms of financial insurance.

Management structure—in the sense of centralization versus decentralization—has risk management overtones. While decentralization of management authority can accelerate critical decision-making, some decision-making needs to be more closely held "at corporate." It has been observed that decentralization of safety functions at BP was a contributor to the Deepwater Horizon disaster.[6] As a related thought, should the environmental engineer at a plant report to (and have compensation set by) the plant manager or to a corporate VP for environmental affairs or both? Should a subsidiary general counsel report to the subsidiary's CEO or to the parent's general counsel or both?

Related to management structure is **staffing**. Risk management needs to be understood as a function, deserving of the right quality and quantity of staffing. Responsibility for leading this function is sometimes placed with the head of internal audit. However, there is a theory that there should be a segregation of duties between those who identify risk (such as an internal auditor) and those who help address risk. As a result, the leader of the team for managing risk is often the chief risk officer or chief compliance officer. Or individuals who share this responsibility can operate together as a committee. Whoever takes the lead will work closely with a general counsel and the person who oversees the insurance program. The stature of the leader or leaders of the function, whom they report to, and the number of people working under them will depend on the complexity of the organization and the risk profile of the company. Finally, the leader or leaders of the function should have a direct line of communication to the board committees charged with taking the lead on oversight of risk and compliance (as discussed below).

Among the responsibilities of the members of management with day-to-day roles in risk management is to provide training about compliance to the broader group of employees—on a periodic basis and as part of onboarding. Subjects will depend upon the business and operations of the company, but will often be embodied in a code of business conduct that will include policies about antidiscrimination, sexual harassment, price-fixing, and other antitrust requirements, securities trading, and the Foreign Corrupt Practices Act. Related to that training, many companies will require employees to periodically certify compliance with company policies and will have the risk management team administer that certification process.

A compliance risk that is often separately managed relates to public disclosure. Following the adoption of Sarbanes-Oxley in 2002, many companies established a disclosure committee comprising a number of members of management, largely from the legal and finance function and sometimes advised by outside counsel. That committee reviews drafts of periodic reports (Forms 10-K and 10-Q) required to be filed with the Securities and Exchange Commission. As part of that process, they review so-called "sub-certifications" from members of management, giving particular attention to any exceptions or concerns raised therein. Sub-certifications are the documents that provide support for the certifications required under Section 302 of Sarbanes-Oxley to be made by the company's "principal executive [CEO] and financial [CFO] officers" about material accuracy and completeness of the reports, the fair presentation of financial information, and the adequacy of the company's internal controls.

Since the Global Financial Crisis of 2008, **compensation design** has received a great deal of attention as an element of risk management. Certainly, a system that incentivizes excessive risk-taking with corporate assets is highly problematic, and risk aspects of compensation design are now required disclosure for public companies.[7] To achieve an appropriate consideration of risk in compensation design, a board's compensation committee should consider meeting annually in executive session, with the most senior members of management tasked with addressing risk.

Beyond general design, a company's compensation clawback policy can also operate as a risk management tool. In the aftermath of Goldman Sachs's legal costs of $5 billion associated with the 1MDB scandal, a good deal of media attention was given to that firm's clawback policy. That policy provided that a clawback of "variable compensation" could be triggered by a "failure to appropriately consider risk" in the "structuring or marketing of any product or service." Individuals covered by the policy were "senior executive officers" who "participated (or otherwise oversaw or [were] responsible for . . .)" such structuring or marketing. In applying the policy, the board of Goldman was reported to seek $174 million from a dozen current and former executives, including the current and former CEOs. To make clawback policies easier to execute, some companies are deferring the payment of bonuses.

But there is another element of risk from compensation that should also be considered—pay equity between men and women employees and between white employees and employees of color. Finally, compensation design can be used to emphasize *desired* elements of corporate culture. For example, if safety or environmental, social, or governance (ESG) goals are an important part of a company's culture, a bonus structure that ties payouts to achieving aspirational targets should be considered.

"War games" (sometimes called "tabletop exercises" or "virtual crises") can be extremely useful in preparing to manage an actual crisis—especially those that may seem to have the highest probability of occurring and that will require the fastest response time to address the crisis and its near-term fallout.

Take, as an example, a food processor. It would make sense for such a company to engage in periodic exercises of dealing with a hypothetical report of serious illness that appears traceable to its products. That exercise would involve convening an appropriate multidisciplinary team under circumstances designed to replicate the stresses of a real crisis—time pressure, inconvenient time, calls from the media or tweets during the meeting, an evolution of known facts, and so on. The team would be pressed to answer questions such as:

- Can we be sure it is our products that caused the illness?
- Can we be sure which facility they come from?
- Should we halt production or issue a warning or recall, even before we have certainty?
- What are we obligated to do as a matter of law?
- Should we notify our insurers?
- Should we pull any TV ads, radio ads, or social media?
- Should we take steps to preserve liquidity?
- What about disclosures under securities laws?
- In the absence of disclosure, would we be able to issue securities and/or should we block insider sales?
- What should we do for our grocery customers . . . and their retail customers?

In advance of engaging in the war game, the following steps should be taken:

- Prepare a list of, and contact information for, the members of management who will be asked to participate.
- Similarly, if outside consultants will be asked to participate, their contact information should be readily available. In fact, it may be desirable for an outside consultant to be hired as a facilitator to develop the hypothetical and to otherwise run the war game.
- Because of the importance of communications, consideration should be given to preparing generic templates of an internal communication, a recall notice, a "holding statement," a public disclosure, a notification to insurers, and (perhaps) a document hold notice. As part of the exercise, the team can modify and complete the templates as appropriate given the hypothetical.

War games can have another salutary effect. By preparing those individuals who will be tapped to deal with the crisis by replicating the stresses, it can take some of the emotion out of managing an actual event. It can be the difference between reacting and responding to the crisis—especially in the "hair on fire" stage. Clear-thinking managers, who nevertheless understand the urgency of a situation, are often better decision-makers. The exercise, while valuable, provides no guarantees, however. To quote Mike Tyson: "Everybody has a plan until they get punched in the mouth."

In the digital age, **information technology** is a key element of risk management. IT failures can be a cause of, or caused by, crisis. This was first observed at the time of the attacks of 9/11. Prior to 9/11, which occurred before the advent of the "cloud," many companies prided themselves on steps they had taken to assure "data recovery." Unfortunately, for some of the companies in the World Trade Center, that meant their backup servers were co-located with, or installed near, the primary servers.

More recently, the risk management aspect of IT relates to cybersecurity. Clearly, companies need to do what they can to prevent cyberattacks (largely though software, "red team" exercises, and employee education), but they also need to know how they are going to mitigate the effects of a successful attack. Discussions around whether or not to pay ransomware, as was done recently in the Colonial Pipeline hack in May 2021, will generate significant debate! While the cloud may have obviated the backup server issue, in the age of ransomware attacks, there is still a need for addressing data recovery and business continuity in IT risk management. A failure to do this can be problematic for public companies, because they have obligations to periodically issue financial statements and ransomware attacks can impact accounting records.

Really well-advised companies are also worried about attacks on professional service firms (lawyers, accountants, and investment bankers) and other types of vendors that are given access to sensitive information. With stay-at-home orders during the Pandemic (much more on this subject in Part VI), IT professionals were presented with a new set of challenges created by having geographically distributed computers accessing a company's proprietary data.

Another tool that is useful for risk management is an effective **whistleblower hotline**. An effective program—one that provides reasonable assurances of confidentiality, anonymity, and non-retaliation—can provide an early warning mechanism about compliance failures, fraud, and excessive or simply unauthorized risk-taking. Because of the role of the board of directors (discussed below), reports of whistleblower complaints should be shared with the board or one or more appropriate committees (typically, the audit committee, a risk committee [if there is one], and sometimes the compensation committee [if it is involved more broadly in human resources]). Similarly, exit interviews of employees in sensitive positions (e.g., an internal auditor) can be useful and any concerns raised in those interviews should be shared with the board. Concerns raised on a hotline or at an exit interview must, however, be appropriately followed up on, lest they set up a later narrative of a failure to address "red flags." Finally, a board should be informed of any special compensation paid to a departing employee if agreed to following a threat by the employee of litigation.

All of the foregoing elements of traditional risk management are described as things that the company should be doing. But, similar to the question we ask in the next chapter about who will manage the crisis, there needs to be a thoughtful answer to the question "Who bears responsibility for risk management?" Certainly, risk is something for the management team, under the leadership of the CEO, to take primary responsibility for. That said, the board of directors has a clear fiduciary duty to oversee the management of a risk—at least the risk of compliance failure.

As with many legal matters, there are two ways to discuss this fiduciary duty of risk oversight—a short version and (for the readers who are lawyers and those readers who are directors and officers and are interested in greater detail) a long version. The short version is this: in 1996, the Delaware courts announced a heightened expectation about directors' obligations in the area of overseeing corporate risk. Starting with compliance risk, the courts held that boards have an obligation, first, to make sure their company has in place a system that will allow the directors to oversee how the management team addresses risk and, second, to oversee the operation of that system. This decision and others that followed have given rise to what are known as "Caremark claims" (for the name of the company involved in that first case). Since then, there has been an arguable expansion of this expectation beyond compliance risk. That's the short version; what follows is the long version.

In a trial court decision in *Caremark*,[8] Delaware chancellor William Allen "reassessed" (a polite term for urging that a precedent be overruled) the holding in a 1963 Delaware Supreme Court decision (*Graham v. Allis-Chalmers*).[9] The earlier case pertained to the obligation of a board to affirmatively engage in oversight about a company's compliance with law. *Graham* held that "absent cause for suspicion there is no duty upon the directors to install and operate a corporate system of espionage to ferret out wrongdoing which they have no reason to suspect exists." In *Caremark*, Chancellor Allen in essence said that times had changed. While "dicta" (i.e., language not needed for the decision and thus without the precedential impact of a "holding"), the chancellor wrote that "it is important that the board exercise a good faith judgment that the corporation's information and reporting system is in concept and design adequate to assure the board that appropriate information will come to its attention in a timely manner." A decade later, the Delaware Supreme Court approved the *Caremark* standard in *Stone v. Ritter*,[10] with something of an extension. Liability can be established not only by a failure to implement a good reporting system. There can also be liability "having implemented such a system . . . [by] consciously fail[ing] to monitor or oversee its operations."

Despite the pronouncements of *Caremark* and *Stone v. Ritter*, for a long time afterward there were very few notable cases about compliance risk oversight. This was, no doubt, because the courts made it clear that it was very difficult to prove a failure of good faith on the part of directors. (That was a good thing for many reasons, not the least of which is that a breach of the duty of good faith is not covered by the exculpatory charter provisions that protect corporate board members.) But in 2019, there were two notable cases in which the courts declined to grant the defendants' motions to dismiss. The first of those cases was a Delaware Supreme Court decision in *Marchand*;[11] the second was a Chancery decision in *Clovis*.[12] Both cases involved "monoline" (or single-product) companies—ice cream and oncology drugs, respectively—where regulatory compliance was determined to be "mission critical."

In the 2020 case of *Hughes v. Hu*,[13] the Delaware Chancery Court declined to dismiss a *Caremark* claim where an audit committee allegedly had "chronic deficiencies" in its responses to evidence of material weakness and inadequate internal controls over accounting and financial reporting. This suggests that, for a public company, compliance with regulations regarding accounting and financial reporting is mission critical. Then, in 2021, the Delaware Chancery Court again declined to dismiss a *Caremark* claim, this time against certain directors and officers of Boeing.[14] While the case was triggered by the two 737 MAX crashes six months apart in late 2018 and early 2019, the Court's opinion recited the company's history regarding safety issues, beginning with a general observation that "as the Company grew, its focus on safety . . . fell away." More specifically, the Court noted that "in the early 2000s, Boeing saw a sharp rise in safety violations [and related fines] imposed by the Federal Aviation Administration," the grounding of the 787 Dreamliner due to lithium-ion battery fires, a 777 crash in 2013 and, in 2015, "an unprecedented settlement with the FAA . . . and historic [level] fines" related to safety, among other things. Despite this context, the Court noted that, until after the second of the 737 MAX crashes, "Boeing lacked any formal, board-level process to oversee safety," and that "this stood in contrast to many other companies in the aviation space." The general mandate of the audit committee to address general risk was not sufficient, due to the fact that the committee "did not take on safety specifically." Moreover, the Court noted that "the Board did not have a means of receiving internal complaints about airplane safety" until after the 737 MAX crashes.

All of these cases presented bad facts, especially in terms of alleged board passivity. It might be possible to interpret those decisions as being limited to those facts. But it is, perhaps, more accurate to describe those cases as part of a trend of progressively increasing expectations of director oversight. If nothing else, the cases support the view that, at least under certain circumstances, risk management related to regulatory compliance is a legal, not just a business, imperative.[15]

Caremark and subsequent cases established a duty of board oversight pertaining to legal compliance risk. After the housing bubble led to the Great Recession and the Global Financial Crisis of 2008, shareholders attempted to expand the duty of oversight to apply to business risk. Plaintiff shareholders of Citigroup alleged that the directors failed "to properly monitor Citigroup's business risk, specifically its exposure to the subprime mortgage market." In rejecting the application of *Caremark*, the Court of Chancery stated that the plaintiff shareholders were "attempting to hold the director defendants personally liable for making (or allowing to be made) business decisions that, in hindsight, turned out poorly for the Company."[16] The *Citigroup* case (and a later case against the directors of JPMorgan relating to the "London Whale" trading debacle) can be read to stand for the proposition that directors are to be held more accountable as a legal matter for compliance risk than for business risk. There may be some irony in that outcome, and those cases might turn out differently today.

Moreover, the recent attention being given to board risk oversight by institutional shareholders does not seem to adopt the courts' distinction between compliance and business risk. For example, Vanguard (which as of March 31, 2021, had $7.2 *trillion* of assets under management, second only to BlackRock) described risk oversight as one of the "four pillars" of good governance and defined it as "Effective, integrated, and on-going oversight of relevant industry—and company—specific risks."[17] In any event, reputational accountability can be meted out at the corporate ballot box and by the financial press for a failure of board oversight of business risk.

Independent of the fiduciary duty delineated in the *Caremark* line of cases, there is another reason for board oversight of compliance as a part of risk management. A really bad set of facts that results in a crisis can expose a company to criminal exposure. Under the Department of Justice's Justice Manual (formerly known as the US Attorney's Manual), in "determining whether to bring charges, and negotiating plea or other agreements, prosecutors should consider," among other things, "the adequacy and effectiveness of the corporation's compliance program at the time of the offense," and thereafter "any efforts to implement an adequate and effective corporate compliance program or to improve an existing one." Interestingly, the Justice Manual explicitly cites *Caremark* in describing an adequate and effective compliance program. On the other hand, if a company is charged and gets convicted (by a court, a jury, or a guilty plea), the presence of an "effective compliance and ethics program" will be treated as a mitigating factor that will reduce the fines that would otherwise be levied on the company. Such a program has the following attribute, among others: "The organization's governing authority [i.e., board] shall be knowledgeable about the content and operation of the compliance and ethics program and shall exercise reasonable oversight with respect to the implementation and effectiveness of the compliance and ethics program."[18]

Perhaps the final reason for board involvement in risk management is "institutional memory." At a time of relatively short CEO tenures (by some reports the median tenure is a mere five years), a number of the board members are more likely than the CEO to have been around during any prior crisis that the company might have gone through. Thus, the board may be a more reliable repository of the lessons learned about the root cause of a company's prior crisis and the lessons learned from how it was handled. (See Chapters 10 and 12.) Moreover, the board may be more attuned to the need for diligence in following up on steps that were identified as appropriate to prevent a recurrence of any similar crisis.

A key governance issue is where, within the board, does responsibility for general risk management oversight reside? Some companies have formal "risk committees." These committees are mostly found in financial institutions and mostly cover financial risk. Other companies seem to default to placing risk management in the audit committee charter. The best approach is to recognize that different committees should address the different risks delineated above. However, as indicated by *Marchand*, "mission critical" compliance risks are sufficiently important that either the full board or a specially designated standing committee should address them.

To be clear, the role of the board is to oversee how the management team addresses risk. There is always the potential for a board to "cross the line" and move from oversight to direct management, and there are no doubt CEOs who feel that their boards do just that. On occasion, we have heard this complaint—especially involving audit committees considering cybersecurity. That said, in doing research for another book, we received this interesting comment from a CEO—"Good governance processes, combined with an aligned board, contribute to minimizing enterprise risk, which in turn frees up this CEO to lead and focus on long-term sustainability and success of the company."

Before leaving the subject of risk management, a thought about risk on a more transactional basis. Risk is to be managed and understood, not totally avoided. There is risk associated with the pursuit of just about any reward in business. Not every effort at innovation, change in product line, plant expansion, acquisition, or personnel decision works out as planned. One of the most important concepts in corporate law is the Business Judgment Rule (BJR), which supports the taking of business risk. The BJR stands for the proposition that corporate fiduciaries are not expected to make perfect decisions, just ones that are well thought out and made free of conflicts of interest. And the BJR, when applicable, puts the burden of proof on those challenging the decision. "Well thought out" might involve including, as part of the decision-making process, understanding the risks associated with the path to be taken. What are the risks to the company of taking this action, and do the potential rewards provide reasonable justification for taking those risks? If we do this thing and there is failure after some period of time, what would be the most likely cause of that failure and is there something we can do now to keep that from occurring? (This last question is sometimes called a premortem.)[19] What are the risks of trying to do it, but failing? What are the risks of not doing this or even trying to do it? This series of questions on a transactional basis may not be what people think of as part of traditional risk management, but going through this exercise may be a way of preventing a future crisis.

Anticipatory Disclosure. As we will discuss in Chapter 6, litigation against a company and its directors and officers during a period of crisis can include claims under the securities laws. As a result, preparedness includes what might be labeled "anticipatory disclosure." While this is not typically thought of as an element of traditional risk management, it can have a mitigating effect when it comes to the overall financial impact of a crisis.

There are three places where such disclosure will appear. First, there is the "risk factors" disclosure in a public company's annual report filed under the 1934 Act on SEC Form 10-K (as well as in a Registration Statement filed under the 1933 Act for the sale of securities). Such factors are often divided between risks associated with a company's industry sector or general economic trends and those associated with the specific company. The discussion can go on for pages and pages. Second, there are disclosures, often found in earnings releases, made to take advantage of the "safe harbor" under the securities laws for "forward-looking statements." Third, there is an element of anticipatory disclosure in the "trends and uncertainties" portion of the Management's Discussion and Analysis required to be included in various SEC forms.

In addition to supporting a "we told you so" defense, these disclosures can, on occasion, be instructive to the members of the board as they discharge their duty of oversight. Hopefully, the disclosures will trigger questions from directors like "What are we doing to mitigate those risks?"

These disclosures must be kept up to date. For example, if a competitor is in crisis due to some perhaps unanticipated turn of events, consideration should be given to whether the company's disclosures (and risk management) need to be updated. Or, if the company adopts a new strategy, changes its operations or capital structure in a material way, or completes a material acquisition, the disclosures (and risk management) may need to change.

Reputation Management. Another nontraditional element of preparedness is reputation management. Reputation has been called a "company's most valuable asset" and warrants proactive, thoughtful management.[20] On a day-to-day basis, reputation matters a great deal to certain current and prospective key constituencies—equity investors, debt funding sources, suppliers, customers, employees, regulators, and legislators. For some consumer-facing companies, reputation is critical for securing and keeping high-value celebrity and other endorsements. (And the reputation of those endorsers also warrants careful attention; think about the number of advertisements featuring Tiger Woods that were pulled in 2009 and 2010.) But consider the parable of the elephant and the blind men; each constituency may have a different perspective. In a time of crisis—especially one that is self-inflicted (Category #1 or #2)—overall reputation can affect how those key constituencies and, importantly, also regulators and juries act toward and think about the company in crisis. In short, a good reputation may allow the company in crisis to catch something of a break. And a reputation for truthfulness may enhance the credibility of crisis-time communications.

So, what are the elements of reputation management? As the subtitle of Daniel Diermeier's excellent book indicates, it is about *building* reputation, and not just the managing of reputational risk. Diermeier gives a number of important insights about this effort:

- "Reputation management . . . [is] based on principled leadership and supported by sophisticated processes and capabilities that are integrated with the company's business strategy and culture."[21]
- "Reputation management should never be delegated to specialists," such as those in public relations and legal functions.[22] Note: even your authors agree with this!
- "Ultimate accountability" for reputation management processes should be placed "at a level of the organization whose job description is the long-term viability of the company: the board."[23]

In keeping with this last notion, one pair of commentators have gone so far as to suggest that boards form a standing committee called an "integrated reputation governance committee" that includes "directors with informational and behavioral economics, behavioral sciences and communications" backgrounds.[24]

Reputation can be derived from words and/or deeds.

A corporation's reputation-building words are often embodied in mission statements or otherwise publicized on websites. In a study of S&P 500 corporations' "advertised values," it was reported that 52 percent listed "integrity" and another 34 percent coupled that with "ethics."[25] When a company has a crisis that belies the advertised values, the plaintiff's bar can bring a class action claiming securities fraud. For example, Goldman Sachs's assertion that "our clients' interests always come first" was challenged after the "ABACUS" collateralized debt obligation problem that allegedly involved a Goldman conflict of interest.[26] It may be a good idea to phrase value statements in a way to be sure they are seen as clearly aspirational—"we strive to . . ."

Especially at the date of this writing, US public company actions that are being used to burnish the corporate reputation are captured in the acronyms CSR (corporate social responsibility) and ESG (environmental, social, and governance). *Real* CSR/ESG involves doing more for the

non-shareholder stakeholders (the "other constituencies") than is required by law, regulation, and contract—even though there is quite a lot
required by those matters! *Dramatic* CSR/ESG might involve encourag-
ing the government to adopt regulations that benefit other constituencies so that, in the words of the president of Microsoft, the marketplace
does not become "a race to the bottom." (He was advocating for regulatory controls over privacy, encryption, artificial intelligence, and content
monitoring.)[27] As a legal matter, actions undertaken in the name of CSR/
ESG can be justified so long as there is any rational connection to the
long-term benefit of the shareholders.

In addition, a savvy public company will have a world-class program of
institutional shareholder engagement of the type advocated for by Black-
Rock.[28] Establishing a relationship and credibility with major shareholders on a "clear day" (while complying with the requirements of SEC Regulation FD [described in Chapter 5] not to engage in selective disclosure)
will yield benefits at a time of crisis.

Shareholder Activism. Because a crisis can trigger an attack by shareholder activists, preparedness for such an attack is critical. Shareholder
activists come in three different orientations—governance, CSR/ESG, and
financial—although there is a degree of symbiosis among those orientations. The success of governance activists in dismantling structural
defenses (e.g., a ban on the call of special shareholders meetings by shareholders) has enhanced the ability of financial activists to win proxy contests or to achieve successful settlements. Moreover, some individual activists show an interest in more than one category. For example, BlackRock
is both a governance and a CSR activist. Jeffrey Ubben, a financial activist
at ValueAct, is now at a different hedge fund and advocating CSR/ESG issues. At the 2021 Exxon annual meeting, the hedge fund Engine No. 1 won
three board seats in a proxy contest in which it advocated a strategic shift
away from fossil fuels.

When a company is in crisis, an attack can focus on causing or "allowing" the crisis to occur or on how the crisis is being handled. The targets
of the attack can be the CEO or members of the board or a particular
committee. One scenario for such an attack can be a proxy contest in
which the dissident advocates for replacing incumbent directors with candidates who will make a change in the CEO. A version of that approach
is to seek to seat someone on the board who is a "CEO-in-waiting." In
light of this, an element of preparedness (which is also a governance best
practice) is emergency succession planning. Another scenario is a withhold vote campaign targeting one or more members of the board. (For
example, in reaction to the $5.5 billion loss at Credit Suisse resulting from

the Archegos Capital Management debacle, shareholders said they would vote against the chair of the risk committee and the lead independent director.) If the influential proxy advisory firm ISS recommends that institutions withhold votes, and if a company has adopted some form of majority voting, this kind of attack can be quite consequential.

Because of all of this, preparedness for shareholder activism is an element of risk management (and, again, a governance best practice). To be generally prepared for shareholder activism, a company should do the following:

- Adopt enhanced advance notice bylaws. These are provisions designed to give an "early warning" before a proxy contest and to require additional information about a number of subjects, including a shareholder's derivative positions.
- Have a full defense team assembled before the commencement of an attack. The outside advisors on the team should include a financial advisor, legal counsel, special situations PR consultants, special situation proxy solicitors, and a stock watch service.
- Engage in a vulnerability assessment. Under normal (that is, noncrisis) circumstances, that means understanding what vulnerabilities about the company and potentially targeted directors a dissident would use in making its case to other shareholders.
- Have a robust shareholder engagement program. Some institutional shareholders have asserted that they wish to have direct access to board members—especially if the company has had governance issues (for example, access to the chair of the compensation committee if there has been a failed say-on-pay vote). At a minimum, the company should have excellent outreach to major shareholders by its investor relations team.
- Be prepared for how to handle an initial call from a potential activist.
- Monitor stock ownership for activists (individual or a "wolf pack").

This general preparation will need to be modified or refreshed when an activist appears on the horizon in the course of a crisis.

* * *

These multiple concrete elements of preparedness will enhance the ability of a company and its team to execute effective crisis management when the time comes to do so. That is the subject of Part II.

3

What Is the Role
of Corporate Culture?

In any type of entity—public companies certainly included—culture plays a major role in advancing the mission of the entity, in risk management and in the management of any crisis.[1] What is corporate culture? There are many books and articles on this subject, but a good working definition is this: "a system of values, beliefs and behaviors that shape how things get done within the organization."[2] A corporate culture has elements that pertain to advancing a corporation's mission and creating value and also elements that pertain to risk management. External perceptions of culture factor into overall reputation—for good or ill.

A culture of collaboration and collegiality can advance the mission of a corporation that provides professional or other services. It assists in the recruiting and retention of talent and helps that talent deliver the best advice. A culture of cooperation and transparency with regulators can advance the mission of companies in highly regulated industries. A culture of innovation can advance the mission of a technology or pharmaceutical company. A culture of striving for operational efficiency and excellence and dealing fairly with employees, customers, and suppliers can advance the mission of just about any company. So can a culture of ambition in striving for aspirational goals, so long as it is tempered by a realistic view of financial and other limitations.

There are myriad elements of corporate culture that pertain to risk management. For just about any company, risk is mitigated by a culture of complying with law and regulation, as well as a culture of respect for individual employees. A culture that values candor and veracity in communicating with all stakeholders is also a general risk mitigant. Finally, a culture of internal candor—especially one that encourages delivering even unwelcome news to one's boss—can be extremely useful as an element of risk management. And useful not just to the company, but also to the boss—who, after all, will be assumed to "have known."

For companies in specific lines of business, there can be cultural values that are particularly important to risk management. For a manufacturer of products that have the potential for causing harm if they fail, a culture that places customer and consumer safety at the forefront is critical. If the manufacturing process itself can injure those making the products, a culture that emphasizes worker safety is also critical. For a public utility, a culture that emphasizes reliability and safety (through high standards for worker training and infrastructure maintenance and otherwise) is an absolute necessity.

When the core operations of a business are focused on one particular skill set—for example, engineering for some companies or trading for some financial institutions—there is a risk that pride in the reputation of that area of the organization can lead to hubris, which can lead to undue risk. Thus, such an organization may need to emphasize a culture of collaboration that empowers all disciplines and does not turn a blind eye to possible excesses of the core.

There is a related point that has been identified by Edgar Schein in his classic book *Organizational Culture and Leadership*. As an organization becomes successful and grows, "it inevitably creates smaller units that begin the process of culture formation on their own."[3] In other words, a complex organization can have subcultures. Care should be taken that there is a consistency and alignment of these subcultures with the overall enterprise when it comes to risk management.

So, how is a positive, risk-mitigating culture established? First, and perhaps foremost, there is the "tone at the top"—namely, the words and actions of the CEO and others in significant positions of authority. Those words can be conveyed in a variety of ways. When a CEO speaks to different groups of employees—town hall meetings of all employees, gatherings of top executives, or annual retreats with direct reports—those sessions should not be limited to operational and financial matters. Those meetings provide a not-to-be-wasted opportunity for a CEO to articulate the desired culture in prepared remarks and in answers to questions. Some CEOs send an annual letter to employees to emphasize elements of desired culture. The same messages are conveyed even more formally in documents labeled codes of conduct, codes of business ethics, and similar titles. Those documents are often signed by the CEO and adopted by the board of directors, but when they are issued in glossy brochures or found only on the company website, the messaging can come across as generic boilerplate. Direct messages from a CEO (especially those delivered orally and with conviction) will usually be the most effective and memorable means of providing "tone at the top."

Words alone, without corresponding actions, can make matters worse by displaying hypocrisy. Actions start with personal behavior by senior leaders that is in keeping with the articulated cultural values. Take one example that has played out far too frequently, causing crises for companies. A CEO who is embroiled in #MeToo behavior is a cultural disaster. A CEO who tolerates that kind of behavior among his or her team is equally damaging to the culture. A variant of this problem is the CEO who fires the miscreant but presides over an excessive, inappropriate severance payment. Another example: a CEO who "shoots the messenger" when a member of the team delivers unwelcome news is giving the message to the rest of the team that internal candor is not valued and is setting up the company (and perhaps himself or herself) for a crisis.

One of the most vivid examples of a disconnect between senior executives' words and actions was provided by Enron. The Enron Code of Conduct was forwarded to all employees by founder, chairman, and former CEO Ken Lay with a memo dated July 1, 2000, that declared "we are all responsible for conducting the affairs of the Company in accordance with all applicable laws and in a moral and honest manner." Shortly after that date, the Enron stock price peaked at over $90 per share. By the end of the following year, Enron had filed for bankruptcy. In 2004, Ken Lay and his successor CEO Jeff Skilling were indicted. In 2006, they were both convicted of fraud. Lay died before his appeals were exhausted, resulting in his conviction being vacated. Skilling was sentenced to 24 years in prison and served 12 years before being released to a halfway house for one more year. In a related SEC proceeding, he was permanently barred from serving as an officer or director of a public company. There is a robust market for Enron memorabilia, although the "Vision and Values" Lucite cube paperweight is reportedly sold out on wallstreettreasures.com.

Then there is the role of the board in corporate culture. A board is now expected to provide oversight of culture. As part of an annual board self-evaluation process, it should consider whether it is satisfied with its own engagement on this subject, whether that engagement is through the board as a whole or its human resources/compensation committee. It can provide oversight, while still honoring the appropriate line between itself and the management team, by using a number of tools. Whistleblower hotline complaints and reports on exit interviews can be illuminating about culture. Seeing what is posted on social media about the company and websites such as Glassdoor might provide worthwhile information. (Note that we say "might," because there tends to be something of an adverse selection of those who post.) For a company in a regulated industry, the tone of communications to and from the regulators might be revealing of culture. A board should think about its own firsthand observations of the CEO and of the interactions between the CEO and the team and among the members of the team. Finally, if there are chronic, recurring problems in certain areas (such as injuries to consumers or employees), that may be a signal that an articulated value is just words.

One final thought about corporate culture: in addition to the working definition noted above, the culture of a corporation involves how employees feel about the place. Among other things, are they proud to be associated with the company? The underlying facts that have created the crisis (especially in Category #1 or #2) can have a significant negative impact on this aspect of corporate culture. Related criminal actions against the company or any of its employees can be particularly bruising. How well or badly the crisis has been managed (regardless of Category) can have a positive or negative impact. For these reasons, during the execution phase to be discussed in Part II, we emphasize communication to employees and the HR aspects of crisis management. Similarly, in Part III, where we discuss reputation rehabilitation, we focus on internal as well as external reputation. In some cases, there will be a need for cultural repair.

· II ·

Execute

Taxonomy of crises

Category	Simplified characteristics
#1	Internally generated/core
#2	Internally generated/non-core
#3	Externally generated/core
#4	Disaster

4

Who Calls the Shots?
Governance and
Organizational Aspects

There are a number of important governance and organizational issues to address in order to achieve effective crisis management. What are the respective roles of the board and management? How does the leadership style of the CEO during crisis compare to that style in normal-course business? How do a CEO and board make sure they are getting all required information and receiving the best advice? When either the board or management are making decisions about how to handle the crisis, for whose benefit are they to be made? Finally, will governance change as a result of the resolution of the crisis?

Board/Management Roles. There is a recurring question in corporate governance of "Where do you draw the line?" between the roles of the board and of the management team. The statutes that govern corporations invariably contain language along the lines of "the corporation is to be managed by or under the direction of the board of directors." That language provides precious little guidance for answering the recurring question. The practical—and more useful—answer to the question is that (i) day-to-day operations are vested in the management team, (ii) certain matters are in the exclusive purview of the board of directors, but they benefit from and should receive the input of the management team, and (iii) some subjects are shared—such as strategy, which results from an iterative process between the board and management.[1]

Another way of answering the question of "where do you draw the line" is to say "it depends"—how critical and/or material is the decision, does management have any element of conflict of interest, and what is the confidence of the board in the CEO and his or her management team?

This "it depends" analysis is particularly important when it comes to crisis management. By definition (or at least the one we use in this book for what constitutes a crisis), decision-making about managing the crisis is both critical and material. Management may or may not have a conflict, especially if the crisis is to a degree self-inflicted. There is the obvious type of conflict of a CEO/#MeToo crisis. Then there can be a more subtle conflict involved where a crisis arguably should have been prevented (e.g., an acquisition gone bad due to a failure of due diligence and just about any other crisis in Category #1), creating the potential for a CEO and his or her team to be defensive or even somewhat in denial. Even when there is no obvious or subtle conflict, the board may not have full confidence in the management team, because of concerns about the ability of the CEO to lead the team effectively in the context of the crisis. This might be because he or she has never been through a crisis of this magnitude. Or because, when first discussing the situation with the board, he or she may have displayed a degree of panic or, conversely, a lack of urgency or seriousness. Or the CEO may not have the ability to adjust his or her management style to what is required to execute well in a crisis situation. (More on that in a moment.)

Even when there is no obvious or subtle conflict and the board has full confidence in the management to address the crisis, the board should take a very active *oversight* role. This will usually take the form of frequent updating calls and occasional special in-person meetings. Why? First of all, the shareholders (and, on occasion, judges and the government) will expect that. If the handling of the crisis goes badly, the directors will not want to be fairly criticized for having been passive.[2] Second, the directors themselves will (or should) want to be kept well informed and, for reasons of confidentiality and privilege, it is better to do that orally. (As a related matter, great care must be taken in the preparation of any advance materials, note-taking, and drafting of meeting minutes.) Of course, both confidentiality and privilege can be lost if directors (or anyone in attendance at such briefings) succumb to entreaties from the press or are otherwise indiscreet. Third—and most importantly—things change during the crisis. Often board-level decisions will need to be made quickly. Thus, the board will need to be apprised on a real-time basis of facts as they develop so it can make those decisions (or provide advice) thoughtfully but in a timely manner. In addition, the board should be in a position to know when it should insert itself more fully or make a change in the team managing the crisis, or even a change in the leader of the team. As to this last point, a board (through the non-executive chair or lead independent director) should maintain a careful watch over how the CEO is dealing with the stress of the situation and how key constituencies are reacting to the CEO's actions and communications.

On occasion, a board will decide to form an ad hoc or special committee to play this enhanced oversight role. Certainly, if there are board members whose schedules will not allow them to invest time in frequent calls and meetings, this may be a practical necessity. If there are board members who have particular experience or expertise in dealing with a specific type of crisis, they are likely to be playing an enhanced role in advising the management team. As a generalization, however, it is usually preferable for the full board to be engaged in this role, at least in the early stages of a crisis.

Depending upon the circumstances, a board or committee playing an enhanced oversight role might engage its own outside consultants to assist it in that role. While unusual (and potentially cumbersome), this will certainly be the case in the event of any concerns about a management conflict.

The flip side of enhanced oversight by a board is the question that, understandably, gets asked occasionally by an individual director—"should I quit?" That of course is a highly personal decision and can relate to the ability of the individual to deal with stress, as well as time demands. As a possible example of both factors, there were reports that the non-executive chair of the board of Wells Fargo resigned as a way of avoiding having to testify before a Congressional committee.[3] However, to the extent that it is asked because of a concern about personal financial exposure, there are several elements to an answer.

First, leaving after the crisis is underway probably doesn't reduce financial exposure from the fact pattern that led to the crisis. To the extent that there are claims that the crisis was the result of a breach of some fiduciary duty, those who were on the board at the time of the alleged failure will be defendants whether or not they have remained on the board. Leaving the board might reduce a risk of financial exposure due to the *handling* of the crisis, but such claims are rather unusual—especially if great care is exercised in preparing crisis-related public disclosures. Moreover, in most instances, the suite of protections available to directors—those that cut off liability (including exculpatory charter provisions that cut off liability for breaches of the duty of care) and those that shift financial exposure to others (including director and officer [D&O] liability insurance)—as well as the business judgment rule significantly reduce the risk of financial exposure, at least based upon fiduciary duty. Of course, there is always reputational exposure, but that might actually be exacerbated by quitting in the middle of the crisis.

In a very extreme case, quitting could lead to an independent source of exposure for a director. One of the most influential Delaware judges in recent years, Leo Strine, ruled from the bench in memorable terms: "the Monty Python response—and I refer to the scene involving the words 'run away' . . . there are some circumstances in which running away doesn't immunize you. It in fact involves a breach of duty."[4] He offered that view in a case before him where the crisis involved a theft of corporate assets by a CEO, and the directors chose to quit rather than confront the CEO. This is a rare situation, indeed, but Strine's admonition might be applicable in other instances. There is also a risk that the breach of duty could be characterized as one of loyalty, not of care—resulting in a loss of the exculpation protection.

On occasion, a governance-related element of crisis management will be to add new members to a board of directors—individuals who have specific skills and reputations for dealing with either crises in general or the issues that led to a specific crisis. For example, if a crisis resulted from a perceived inadequate attention to safety issues, then an individual known for his or her experience in that arena might be a desirable addition, for both substance and optics. In addition, if the handling of the crisis involves dealing with regulators, a former regulator or a person known for success in dealing with regulators might be sought as an addition to the board. Of course, adding a recently former regulator may raise issues under government ethics rules or trigger "revolving door" articles in the press.

Should such an individual accept the invitation? Because the underlying facts that led to the crisis occurred before joining the board, any hesitation should not be founded on concern with personal financial exposure based upon a claim of breach of fiduciary duty leading to the crisis. However, if there is any sense that the addition of the individual is simply window dressing and that there is not a commitment to engaging in a thorough root cause analysis (discussed in Chapter 10), or making necessary changes or handling the crisis with transparency, professionalism, high-quality advisors, and true concern for those affected by the crisis, then the invitation should be declined. Otherwise, there can be both financial and reputational exposure.

Another reason for adding new members will be to enable the board to empanel a special litigation committee to address shareholder litigation against directors for breach of fiduciary duty. (More on this form of litigation in Chapter 6.) The critical question for an individual being invited for this purpose is whether he or she will qualify as truly independent. This question requires understanding not just a stock exchange's definition of independence. There is a good deal of case law dealing with the independence of members of a special litigation committee. Those cases make it clear that a court will closely scrutinize whether social, philanthropic, business, and other relationships might impede the ability of a director to reach a decision purely in the best interests of the corporation.[5]

In addition to these considerations, an individual invited to join a board under any circumstances should engage in due diligence and ask a series

of other questions of the company and of him-/herself before joining the
board.[6]

- What is the commitment of the CEO to quality corporate governance and does he or she view the directors as valued advisors?
- Is the information provided to the board—both for meetings and
  between meetings—sufficient to allow it to fulfill its fiduciary duties? (Sufficiency being measured in transparency, appropriateness
  of format, and timeliness.)
- What is the quality of the non-executive board chair or lead independent director and does he or she have a partner-like relationship
  with the CEO?
- What is the quality of individuals both inside and outside the company who deal with the critical aspects of being a public company?
- Does the general counsel recognize his or her ethical responsibilities
  to the board?
- What is the atmosphere and culture in the boardroom?
- Is the board appropriately engaged in oversight of risk management,
  in strategy, and in making major decisions?
- Is the board currently populated with quality individuals, with expertise and experience relevant to the challenges and opportunities
  of the company?
- Do I have the time to serve and am I available at the right times?

Role of the CEO. Assuming that the crisis management team will be
directed by the CEO, what does that role entail?

First and foremost (and perhaps most obviously), the role is to provide leadership. A truly effective CEO is much more than just a manager
and is not a leader just because of his or her title and apparent authority.
In the context of crisis management, it is especially important that the
CEO earns and retains the trust and confidence of those being led as well
as the trust and confidence of the other constituencies affected by the crisis. The starting point is to have an excellent reputation before the crisis
begins. Then, during the crisis, the CEO must exhibit excellent judgment,
act diligently, accept responsibility, and communicate internally in a calm,
reflective manner.

It can be difficult for one leading a response to a crisis to display the
requisite degree of calm, because of the stress. And the reminder to the
leader to do so is not likely to come from members of the team, so it may
need to come from a lead independent director who has a good relationship with the CEO. There is a wonderful vignette about Winston Churchill

during the tense times in the lead-up to the war with Germany. His lead independent director was his wife, Clementine. She wrote to the prime minister: "I must confess that I have noticed a deterioration in your manner . . . [you must] combine urbanity, kindness and if possible Olympic calm . . . One leads by calm."[7]

Interestingly, Schein describes a counterintuitive example of leadership in a time of stress. He describes Ken Olsen at Digital Equipment Corporation: "When the company was doing well, [he] often had emotional outbursts . . . When the company was in difficulty, however, [he] never punished anyone or displayed anger: instead, he became the strong and supportive father figure . . ."[8]

There is no more important time for the CEO to provide true leadership (and to attain "followership") than in a time of crisis. The success or failure of efforts to manage a crisis is often inextricably linked to the quality of CEO leadership.

Second, the CEO will need to assemble a multidisciplinary team to deal with the crisis, and also make sure there is another team in place to keep running the business. (Some members of management, like the CEO, will need to do double duty.) The crisis management team should cover the following disciplines: communications (PR and investor relations), legal (disclosure, corporate governance, employment law, and litigation), regulatory (in many cases), finance, operations, and HR. Technology experts may also be needed. The internal resources should be supplemented by outside experts with crisis management experience. In a crisis that creates extreme financial stress, the outsiders may need to include so-called "turnaround" specialists. Both internal and external team members should be selected with an eye toward expertise, experience, and (at least as important) the ability, when under stress, to work in a collaborative manner, to communicate disagreement in a collegial fashion, and to display a calm temperament. The CEO assembling the team may get a preview of these last attributes during war game exercises, described in Chapter 2.

Engagement letters with outside experts should be reviewed with care, starting with the question of whether, for privilege purposes, the engaging party should be legal counsel (internal or outside). The financial terms should also receive a good deal of focus; companies should not abandon normal discipline for controlling costs in such matters simply because of the crisis context. We once heard an outside expert brag that "I was given an unlimited budget . . . and exceeded it!"

On occasion, the internal team members will need to be convinced to accept outside help. And if that acceptance is given begrudgingly, insiders might be tempted to limit access by the outsiders to the CEO (and the board). For substantive reasons and to bolster the confidence level of the board members, outside experts should be full and visible members of the team. This is more likely to occur if the outsiders are respectful of their internal counterparts (and they sometimes need to be coached along these lines).

At the same time, as indicated, the CEO needs to make sure that the normal operations of the company continue to run as smoothly as possible. As in the case of a major M&A transaction, there will be folks who want to be where the action is and may equate being assigned "normal" operations with being relegated to the junior varsity. Nothing could be further from the truth. Aside from sincerely assuring them that that is not the case, the CEO can address this issue by having the two teams meet together from time to time and by advocating for equitable compensation.

One last word on the selection of members of the teams for crisis management and normal operations. A crisis at a company can also be a crisis for one or more individuals—especially those who have, or feel that they have, some responsibility for causing or not preventing the crisis. Such individuals may not be appropriate to serve on either team. Indeed, the best thing for them and for the company may be to put them on paid or unpaid leave. (This is one of the reasons for including HR and an employment lawyer on the crisis management team.)

After assembling the right team, a key role for the CEO will be to act as a facilitator to elicit the best thinking of individual team members and then mediate between differences of opinion on the team. This is no small task, because opinions can be very strongly held and aggressively advocated. To play this role effectively may require the CEO to adopt a leadership style that differs from the style that has worked for him or her under normal business conditions. The exigencies of a crisis may compel a less analytical approach than the CEO normally follows. (This is a particularly bad time for "analysis paralysis.") A crisis may require a commanding style from a CEO who has otherwise been more affiliative or democratic.[9] Perhaps even more than in the case of normal business decisions, it requires the CEO to select from among options based upon merit, not the tenure, title, or status of, or personal relationship with, the person advocating for a particular position. At the same time, the CEO will want to hold the team together and insist on full collaboration. To do this will require the ability to convince those whose ideas did not carry the day that their input was nevertheless valued, that compromised solutions do not always work, and that, ultimately, the goal is to get to the best response and not think in terms of winning and losing.

Of course, a major role for the CEO is in the area of communications. He or she is very likely to be the principal internal and external communicator. Indeed, because of the importance of consistency of messaging and accuracy of disclosure, "principal" may come close to "only." The CEO is likely to be selected for this role because in most instances he or she plays that role whenever something really important is going on with the company—both as a matter of normal corporate protocol and because the CEO is often the person in the company with the best communication skills. If nothing else, when the best crisis communication strategy includes delivering an apology by the company (see Chapter 9), who else is the appropriate messenger? If another officer, or even a director, is assigned the role at the time of crisis, questions might arise about CEO conflicts or cowardice. On the other hand, as will be discussed in Chapters 6 and 7, there can be downsides to putting the CEO in this position.

On occasion, there will be a CEO who, like an individual director, will think about quitting. As is the case with a director who contemplates quitting, this is an intensely personal choice. It may be that the CEO genuinely believes that he or she is not the right person for the job of managing the crisis, is a "lightning rod" for criticism of the company by regulators or shareholders, or has concluded (even before being told) that the board has lost confidence in his or her ability to handle the crisis or to manage the company post-crisis. A mid-crisis change in CEOs is a rare event, but the potential underscores the point made in Chapter 2 about succession planning as a part of crisis preparedness as well as a governance best practice.

When there is a mid-crisis change in CEOs, whether voluntary or involuntary on the part of the predecessor, the new CEO needs to exercise some caution in offering public comments about what has occurred before he or she took office. Backward-looking comments that are critical of the prior regime about how it allowed a crisis to occur or about its management of the crisis can seem self-aggrandizing or, worse, actually damage the company.[10] On the other hand, forward-looking comments about remedial action and/or seeking an improved relationship with regulators and others, while perhaps implicitly critical of the past, may nevertheless be helpful to the ongoing management of the crisis.

Getting Required Information. Quality decision-making, whether in the context of a crisis or otherwise, requires a combination of analysis, judgment, and information. Getting quality information in a crisis can be a challenge. As noted above, there can be a subtle conflict based on corporate politics, competitiveness, or simply personality clashes among members of the management team. That conflict could result in a shading (or worse) of the information supplied to those responsible for managing the crisis. This could lead to poor decisions and inaccurate or incomplete communications. The first step to addressing this issue is to recognize it as a potential problem and to articulate clearly to those who are to provide information the lesson of Watergate—a cover-up can often have consequences that are worse than those of the event being covered up. With this in mind, appropriate steps need to be taken to preserve relevant documents (paper and electronic, or company-owned and personal devices).

But more can be done, as well. All members of the crisis management team should be encouraged (early and often) to provide relevant information in their possession as accurately, completely, and promptly as possible. The bias, too frequently seen in the corporate world, against giving a CEO "bad news" is especially dangerous in the context of a crisis. But the team should also be told, in words that cannot be fairly taken to connote any sinister motive, that providing information should be done in a constructive fashion. For example, accuracy will require a careful delineation, and being explicit, between what is "known" and what is "believed" or even "feared." Moreover, it may be best to deliver the information orally, rather than in writing, especially if the accuracy of the information may be suspect. It may be best to supply the information to company counsel, for purposes of establishing or preserving privilege. But note that just having a lawyer in the room or on the phone or copied on an email will not necessarily be enough to establish privilege. When previously supplied information is learned to have been incorrect or is overtaken by events, providers of that original information should be required to correct or update it promptly. That may require a "no fault" approach. Finally, language used in conveying information—whether orally or in writing—should be professional in tone. Provocative or colorful language is the kind of thing that the press, social media, regulators, and plaintiffs can and will latch on to. That kind of language can be used as an unhelpful "sound bite."

Under certain circumstances, it may be necessary to involve a completely independent third party in information gathering. That retention might best be made through legal counsel and, in any event, the engagement letter warrants a careful review. For example, is the company, its counsel, or the board the party doing the hiring?

When information is being conveyed to the board, consideration should be given to the form of the communication, who is delivering that information, and (again, relevant to privilege) who is in the boardroom or on the phone.

Finally, there needs to be a recognition that, while facts may not actually evolve, an understanding of the facts does evolve. As that understanding develops, decisions may need to change—on occasion, radically so. This is not a sign of weakness or of a "flip-flop." Quite the contrary, it is a reality of crisis management. So, during the course of managing a crisis, it is important to periodically revisit the team's understanding of the facts—"do we *still* think that . . . ?"

An additional and entirely different type of information is needed for those who are managing a crisis—information about what others are saying about the crisis and how it is being handled. "Others" include the press, posters on social media, whistleblowers, the government (Congress, regulators, and prosecutors), securities analysts, and investors. While there can be a negative bias and even inaccuracy in such information, it is nevertheless useful to see how the company and the crisis managers are being perceived by outsiders. One commentator has asserted that "a central precept of crisis management [is] embracing criticism,"[11] and that managers should "reach out to critics."[12] This information should be gathered and periodically provided to management and the board in a timely fashion. In the very early stages of crisis management, "periodically" may be daily. From some sources (e.g., the government), "immediate" might be the correct standard for timeliness.

For Whose Benefit Are Decisions to Be Made? Corporate fiduciaries are to make decisions for the benefit of the corporation and its shareholders. This is true whether the fiduciaries are directors or officers, or whether the company is engaged in business as usual or is in crisis. That said, decisions can be made that serve the short-term interests of nonshareholder constituencies so long as the board and management reasonably believe that there is a long-term benefit for the shareholders. So long as the board and management are free of conflicts of interest relating to such decisions, this will be the legal basis supporting a variety of actions. In a crisis, this may include actions such as generous retention bonuses for employees who might be getting calls from competitors, charitable contributions to communities affected by the crisis, and no-questions-asked refunds paid to customers.

If the crisis puts the company into perilous financial straits, questions may nevertheless arise as to whom the directors and officers owe their fiduciary duties. This has been a confusing area of corporate law. Do directors of an insolvent corporation owe fiduciary duties to its creditors, who (at the end of the day) may become the shareholders? The Delaware courts have meandered about over time when addressing this question. In 1944, the Delaware Supreme Court held that, upon insolvency, the duties of directors shifted to the creditors. In 1991, Chancellor Allen in *Credit Lyonnais* stated that directors owe duties to creditors, as well as to the shareholders, when the company enters the "vicinity of insolvency." Then, in 2007, the Delaware courts held that "as a practical matter . . . directors never owe fiduciary duties directly to creditors," but that creditors have shareholder-like standing to pursue derivative claims against directors on behalf of the corporation whenever the company is insolvent or in the "zone."[13]

Post-Crisis Governance. When the crisis is over (or mostly over), there will sometimes be changes in governance—either voluntarily adopted or imposed as part of litigation settlements or the resolution of a bankruptcy proceeding. Voluntary changes in governance and organization will be discussed in Chapter 11. Of course, the most significant governance change might be terminating the CEO (see Chapter 8) or stripping a CEO who is also the board chair of that title and role. (Indeed, this may occur mid-crisis.) Involuntary changes—especially in governance—can be baked into settlement agreements, either with private (often class action) litigants or with regulators (including the SEC) or the Department of Justice. The most expensive and invasive of such changes involve the appointment of a corporate monitor (see Chapter 6).

5

Can We Afford This?
Financial Aspects

Crises can cause massive, and even frightening, disruption to the company's financial attributes (earnings, cash flow, liquidity, and balance sheet) and to the market value of its securities. In an extreme case, a company in crisis may need to file for bankruptcy.

Corporations fund their operations, capital expenditures, and dividends from multiple sources: cash on hand; new cash flow from sales of goods and services; payment terms from suppliers of raw materials, component parts, and vital services; debt in the form of bonds, commercial paper, and bank loans; and equity investments. When a company is in crisis, in a worst-case scenario, it may experience a financial, or more accurately liquidity, double whammy.

Whammy #1: A company will need additional funding to cover the expense of crisis management, to remedy or eliminate the cause of the crisis, to compensate third parties affected by the crisis (to the extent insurance is not sufficient or paid out in a timely fashion) and, possibly, to pay fines.

Whammy #2: At the same time, its normal sources of funding may become constrained or become more expensive. For example, the crisis may adversely impact sales and, thus, cash flow from operations. Nervous suppliers may put the company on a cash on delivery (COD) basis. Bonds or commercial paper may be downgraded by rating agencies and, thus, new issuances or refunding will require a higher rate of interest in order to compensate lenders for taking greater risk of non-repayment. (A downgrade might also trigger a requirement to provide collateral.) New borrowings or other capital raises might even become impossible for some period of time if the crisis impacts the ability to issue financial statements or if the markets feel sufficiently skittish about the prospects for the company. The company may not be able to issue a borrowing certificate under its bank credit agreement, because such a certificate typically states that many of the representations and warranties in the agreement (possibly including no material adverse change and no material litigation or compliance

failures) are true and correct at the date of each borrowing. If a crisis com-
pels the establishment of significant accounting reserves, the company
may not be able to meet existing debt covenants based upon financial
ratios and debt may be accelerated and even cause cross-defaults. Under
circumstances such as these, new equity funding, including through a so-
called PIPE (private investment in public equity) transaction—typically
thought of as the most expensive form of financing—may become extraordinarily dilutive to existing shareholders, if available at all.

And all of this may be exacerbated by SEC disclosure rules—principally, the Management's Discussion and Analysis (MD&A), which requires
that a company report in its quarterly Form 10-Q and its annual Form 10-K
about (among other things) its "liquidity and capital resources."[1] More
than one CEO has noted that complying with those rules creates a self-
fulfilling prophecy. That is, the CEO will say to his or her securities lawyers that a disclosure about a possible liquidity risk will cause suppliers to
put the company on COD terms and, thereby, cause the risk to come to
fruition to the detriment of shareholder value. This is one of those issues
that can cause significant friction within the crisis management team, because under certain circumstances securities lawyers cannot give disclosure advice and simply shrug if the CEO (or another member of management) who receives the advice declines to follow it. As a matter of SEC
practice since the 1980s,[2] as a matter of professional responsibility,[3] and
as required by Sarbanes-Oxley,[4] if a CEO fails to follow disclosure advice
and if the lawyer believes the failure would result in a material violation of
law or is likely to result in substantial injury to the company, then the lawyer will be obligated to go "up the ladder"—that is, raise the issue with the
board of directors of the company—and perhaps even take other actions.
On top of all of that, the auditors issuing opinions on a company's financial statements will need to modify that opinion with a "going concern"
condition if there is an issue as to liquidity in the subsequent 12 months
or some other condition.[5] Some forms of modified opinion can be a credit
agreement default.

So, how do a company and its crisis managers deal with all of this? The
initial steps are to be taken before the crisis occurs. As indicated in Chapter 2, risk management should include financial stress testing. While this
is a useful exercise, it has limits. It can be difficult to predict the magnitude of the potential liquidity impact of an even somewhat predictable
crisis. The impact of a crisis on liquidity may differ depending upon when
in a company's business cycle, or even when during the year, the crisis
manifests. And, in a pre-crisis period, a company may have been pressured by shareholders to reduce its "rainy day" liquidity cushion and buy
back stock or otherwise to maintain a "more efficient" balance sheet.

After the crisis hits, it is critical to focus on maintaining good relationships with all of those who can have an impact on the ability of a company to weather the storm. Non-alarmist and timely transparency with lenders, key suppliers, and other important business partners may result in having them cooperate with the company during its time of difficulty. But remember that the relationship person at each such entity may have to convince, and answer to, an internal constituency when advocating for cooperating with a company in crisis.

Remember, too, that those communications made in the name of transparency must also be in compliance with the SEC's Regulation FD. That regulation was adopted by the SEC in the year 2000, and it is designed to prevent "selective disclosure." In essence, it prohibits sharing information before it has become public with certain types of individuals if the information is "material"—that is, information that has not yet been disclosed and is what a reasonable investor would take into account in deciding to buy, sell, or hold securities. Information that a company is learning about as a crisis unfolds may be material, but not yet sufficiently verified or understood for purposes of being broadly disseminated. Nevertheless, it might be the type of information that, with appropriate caveats, would be shared in the name of transparency. The types of people covered by the regulation are securities professionals and current security holders "under circumstances in which it is reasonably foreseeable that the person will purchase or sell the issuer's securities on the basis of that information." There are exclusions and exceptions, including if the person with whom the information is being shared "expressly agrees to maintain the disclosed information in confidence." That agreement may be oral, although there can be issues of proof if it is not in writing. The agreement need not also expressly prohibit trading, although cautious companies will often add that as a requirement. On occasion, executives will cite Regulation FD in declining to answer press inquiries, even though the media is not covered by the rule.

Cooperation by lenders can come in a couple of different forms. A lender may "forbear" from exercising certain rights in return for concessions of one kind or another. This leaves the default in place, which could cause a cross-default under other debt instruments. Or, a lender may agree to "amend and extend" to eliminate the default and extend the term of the loan. One of the concessions that may be required to achieve either outcome may be for the borrower to secure a previously unsecured loan or to grant additional collateral to an already secured lender. Negotiations relating to the grant of collateral can be complicated by the potential impact on other debt of the company. In addition, a lender receiving new collateral will be concerned about "preference risk" if the company were to file for bankruptcy within 90 days following such receipt. A company granting collateral must recognize that by doing so, its lender will have greatly increased its leverage in any future negotiation.

A possible alternative to dealing with existing lenders is to access sophisticated, non-bank credit markets that have developed in recent years and that supply capital to even distressed companies, although that market will typically demand collateral or contemplate an equity-for-debt swap. A board of directors should understand and consider the full implications of, and alternatives to, the approach it selects. Its deliberations and rationale should be carefully documented.

A similar approach with outside auditors of timely transparency may not obviate a going concern opinion, but will still be important. Anyone who deals with the auditors at any time, but especially in times of crisis, should be aware of the SEC prohibition on exercising "improper influence on the conduct of audits," which can cover (among other things) providing an auditor "with an inaccurate or misleading legal analysis" (as will be relevant to establishing reserves) or "inadequate or misleading information that is key to the audit."[6]

More concrete steps to preserving liquidity may include any or all of the following:

- Preemptively drawing down bank lines before it becomes impossible to issue an unqualified borrowing certificate.
- Stretching payment terms with trade creditors.
- Suspending the payment of dividends and stock buybacks. (As discussed below, this may be required or provided anyway as a matter of corporate law and/or the law against fraudulent transfers.) Note that eliminating dividends may require some institutional investors to sell their positions, putting pressure on the stock price.
- Hiring freezes, employee layoffs, and/or compensation changes, including reducing or suspending 401(k) matching (see Chapter 8).
- Canceling, deferring, or pausing capital expenditure projects, including acquisitions (all possibly subject to contractual obligations).
- Selling assets, including business units.
- Negotiating settlements that provide for payments to claimants or the payment of fines in installments, over time.

At a very early stage in a crisis, the board should be presented with a very thorough analysis of potential financial and liquidity consequences (likely under different scenarios). Keep in mind, however, that such an analysis might have relevance to MD&A and other disclosures. Board oversight of the financial aspects of a crisis should include a fresh look at projections, sometimes with the assistance of specialized financial consultants. For example, will expenses increase to deal with the crisis and/ or is the crisis of a nature that will negatively impact sales? That fresh look may lead to withdrawing earnings guidance that has previously been provided to analysts. (Again, a withdrawal will need to be Reg. FD compliant.) It may be appropriate to take an enhanced look at cash flow projections—enhanced in the sense of understanding funding needs on a more frequent than normal basis, perhaps even monthly. Financing sources may demand to see those projections as well.

Whether as a result of MD&A disclosure, a going concern opinion, the withdrawal of earnings guidance, the elimination or reduction of dividends, or just the notoriety of the crisis, a company dealing with a crisis may also have to deal with the impact of short sellers. (Short sellers borrow stock, sell it, and buy shares at a later date to return them to the party that loaned them the shares.) There is an argument to be made that short sellers have a useful function to perform in the securities markets. Nevertheless, many companies have experienced what they believe to be a "bear raid"—that is, investors with short positions who foment rumors or amplify the negative aspects of a company's disclosures in order to drive down the price of a stock and, thus, increase the ultimate profitability of their short positions. A company in crisis may be especially vulnerable to this kind of activity. If, as a result of aggressive short selling or otherwise, a company's stock were to decline to below $1.00 per share for 30 consecutive trading days, the stock exchange could initiate a delisting process. A company can forestall that process through a reverse stock split.

A significant decline in the price of the company's stock can lead to an unsolicited and opportunistic takeover proposal. As a result, the board of a company in crisis may wish to consider adopting a shareholders rights plan (aka a "poison pill"), or at least having one "on the shelf" for adoption quickly when and if needed. (A "poison pill" is a structural takeover defense that can be put in place by a corporate board without shareholder approval and can only be removed by a board. It deters a bidder from acquiring more than a certain percentage of outstanding stock directly from the shareholders in a tender offer unless it has received the advance consent of the board. This is because if it were to do so, the bidder would experience massive dilution of the value of the shares it owns and those being acquired.) One of the critical variables in the terms of such a device is the triggering percentage—that is, what level of unwanted stock ownership would cause the pill to release its poison and, thus, deter anyone from exceeding that percentage. While most pills utilize a 10, 15, or 20 percent trigger, if the crisis has the effect of creating a large net operating loss (NOL) for tax purposes, the board of such a company will want to consider a so-called "382 pill" (named for the relevant Internal Revenue Code section); such a pill has a 5 percent trigger, designed to prevent the erosion of the value of the NOL.

Sometimes the combined impacts of increased costs, the loss of ability to fully fund both normal operations and the crisis, an inability to estimate with any degree of confidence the full cost of settling litigation related to the facts underlying the crisis, and inadequacy of steps that might preserve liquidity will lead to a conclusion that the only realistic way to deal with the financial aspects of a crisis is to seek to reorganize the company under Chapter 11 of the federal bankruptcy statute. (A crisis with a literally existential impact may lead to a liquidation under Chapter 7 of that statute.) While it is hard to generalize the conditions that lead a company to file under Chapter 11 in conjunction with a crisis, this has frequently been the outcome in the case of crises caused by industry disruption (e.g., post-internet retail), industry-wide financial challenges (e.g., oil/energy), and mass torts (e.g., asbestos).

In the case of mass torts, this is for several reasons. First, a bankruptcy filing will cause all litigation to be placed on hold (i.e., a "stay"). Second, when there are both significant claims by current victims and the *potential* for significant claims by future victims, a bankruptcy filing will allow for a fair process where counsel for current claimants will negotiate with a court-designated representative of the "futures," resulting in an allocation of assets (cash and equity) to be placed in trust. While a trust of that sort could be established without a filing, it is only in a bankruptcy that a "channeling injunction" can be issued, limiting the payouts to the current and future claimants to what has been placed in the trust.

There is one implication of a bankruptcy filing that may be pertinent especially (but not exclusively) in a bankruptcy resulting from a crisis involving mass torts. Dividend payments or stock repurchases made when a company is insolvent might be characterized as improper under the applicable corporate statute or as a fraudulent transfer under various other state or federal statutes. For example, under the Delaware corporate statute, repurchases may not be made by a company if its capital is "impaired" or would become impaired as a result of the repurchase. The statute also provides that dividends can only be paid out of "legally available funds." A willful or negligent violation of those requirements by a director can subject that director to liability to the corporation and its creditors for six years thereafter. Fortunately, Section 172 of the statute also provides that a director "shall be fully protected in relying in good faith upon the records of the corporation and upon such information [etc.] . . . presented to the corporation by [officers, experts] . . . [regarding] . . . funds from which dividends might be properly declared and paid, or with which the corporation's stock might properly be purchased or redeemed." If the dividend payments or stock repurchases are characterized as a fraudulent transfer under state or federal laws, then under some circumstances, recovery can be made from transferees of the improperly transferred funds. So, when a company files bankruptcy, the creditors (or, if one has been appointed, the trustee) can attempt to recover from the directors or certain of the transferees. To do so, they must establish that at the time of the dividend or repurchase, the company was effectively insolvent, even though the bankruptcy filing took place later. And to recover against the directors, they must establish that either they did not receive the kind of information called for by Section 172 or did receive it but did not rely on that information in good faith. In pursuing such claims, the creditors (or trustee) will pore over emails and other documents generated from the outset of the crisis, looking for something that can be used to suggest that the company was aware at an early date of the existential threat posed by the crisis. In accounting parlance, the exercise would be to establish that there should have been reserves set up under FAS 5 (ASC 450-20). That pronouncement covers "loss contingencies" and can require reserves even for claims that have not yet been unasserted, so long as (i) those claims are probable of assertion, (ii) an unfavorable outcome is probable, and (iii) the amount of loss can be reasonably estimated.

Of course, a bankruptcy filing has other implications. In most cases, the management and board of the company will stay in place (the so-called "debtor in possession") and it will be able to attract emergency financing ("DIP financing"). A company can grant to a DIP lender certain protections and other benefits that are not available outside a bankruptcy. While management and the board will be able to continue to make business-as-usual decisions, any decisions of a material nature (such as a sale of assets) will require court approval. For a certain period of time, existing management and the board will have the exclusive right to propose a plan of reorganization. Under unusual circumstances, however, a trustee will be appointed with significant powers over the operation of the company. And to obtain approval of a debtor's restructuring plan, it may be necessary to agree to changes in a board and/or management, usually pursuant to negotiations with creditors. For a debtor in a regulated industry, those changes may also be required to obtain the support of its regulator for the terms of the bankruptcy.[7]

The financial aspects of a crisis have greater complexity when they are being addressed simultaneously by more than one—or even all—of the participants in a particular industry. As noted in Chapter 1, does the timing and/or booking of an accounting reserve by one company impact the thinking of another (or of the SEC or the outside auditors)? Moreover, when multiple companies are negotiating a global settlement with, say, 50 states' attorneys general, what will be the impact of the inability or unwillingness of one or more of the companies to step up to their fair share?

6

What About Those Lawyers?
Legal Aspects

In thinking about legal aspects of a crisis, one's thoughts quickly go to defending litigation and, then, to addressing any applicable regulatory concerns. That is natural enough, but the most immediate legal issue in a crisis relates to disclosures. And the other temporal bookend of the crisis from a legal standpoint are settlements, which can take years to achieve and create obligations that go on for years thereafter. Finally, a company in crisis should not be thinking exclusively about defense. There are claims that it should be considering bringing against others.

Disclosure. Upon learning about the facts and circumstances that have led to a crisis (or that may develop into a full-blown crisis), one of the first questions that should be addressed to counsel is "what are our disclosure obligations?" This is a very different question than "strategically, what, when, and how should we be communicating?," which is the subject of Chapter 7. The differences between required disclosure and strategic communications can lead to very interesting conversations between folks like your co-authors.

Disclosure obligations may arise from a variety of sources.

For a US public company, the starting point in any analysis is the federal securities laws. As a general proposition, there is no obligation to disclose even material non-public information, except when (i) the company is selling or buying its own securities or insiders are trading for their own accounts, (ii) there is a specific requirement of disclosure under an SEC form, or (iii) there has been a leak of such information from the company.

The first of these exceptions is often summarized with the phrase "disclose or abstain." (There is an exception to this exception, if the company or the insider has properly adopted a Rule 10b5-1 plan. [That is a plan under which a company or individuals declare an intention to trade securities periodically at dates in the future, so as to negate the suggestion that trading was motivated by the possession of material non-public information.] If, in the absence of a 10b5-1 plan, individuals do trade before there has been complete and accurate disclosure, they can face potential civil and criminal penalties for insider trading.) The second exception can be triggered by the requirements of SEC Form 8-K, which among other things requires an essentially real-time disclosure of a company's conclusion that "a material charge for impairment to one or more of its assets . . . is required under generally accepted accounting principles." The second exception is even more likely to be triggered, as noted in Chapter 5, by the requirements of the MD&A. As to the third exception, if a company is asked by the press or even a stock exchange about rumors, it can stand on a "no comment" position, but only so long as the rumors did not result from a leak from the company or one of its insiders. (A caveat: the phrase "no corporate developments" is *not* the equivalent of "no comment.") If a rumor did emanate from such a source, then the company will have a disclosure obligation under Regulation FD (discussed above). And, of course, if, thanks to social media, facts are already out in commerce, it can be literally incredible to stick with a no comment position.

When disclosures are made, they must be accurate and complete in all material respects in order to comply with SEC requirements. "Materiality" is defined in subjective terms. And the SEC has cautioned against excessive reliance on quantitative "rules of thumb."[1] An item is material if "it is probable that the judgment of a reasonable person . . . would have been changed or influenced by the inclusion or correction of the item." The words "or influenced by" indicate that, for SEC purposes, the item need not be outcome determinative. In addition to the SEC requirements, there is a corporate law fiduciary duty of candor that applies even when companies are not seeking action (such as a vote) by shareholders. The duty of candor in that context will be breached if directors are found to be "deliberately misinforming shareholders."[2]

After the initial disclosure has been made, there can be obligations to correct or update that disclosure. The most obvious source of such an obligation is if the initial disclosure proves to have been incorrect or misleading. Given how crises play out, with new information emerging regularly and a frequent bias during the "hair on fire" phase to engage in "damage control" or to try to tamp down any panic, that is a distinct possibility. There can also be an obligation to update if a statement is material, forward-looking, and becomes misleading due to a subsequent event. Often companies will expressly note that things change, that the disclosure is as of the date initially made, and that the company is not undertaking to provide real-time updates.

In some rare instances, a crisis will call into question the validity of previously issued financial statements or mandate that they be amended.

If that is the case, Item 4.02 of SEC Form 8-K requires a disclosure to the effect that investors should not rely upon those previously issued statements. If circumstances make it impossible to file required periodic SEC forms (10-K or 10-Q) on time, the company would need to notify investors of that fact and get an extension of the time to file under SEC Rule 12b-25.

Aside from the SEC disclosure requirements, depending upon the type of crisis, a company may have a disclosure obligation under state or federal regulatory requirements. The classic examples are product recall notice requirements administered by the Consumer Product Safety Commission (CPSC) and the Food and Drug Administration (FDA). In addition, there are myriad regulatory requirements for notices of cybersecurity breaches. Such breaches (or even attempted, but foiled, breaches) may also need to be disclosed to clients and customers as a matter of contract law. As part of preparedness planning, a company should understand in detail its disclosure obligations under a variety of possible scenarios—to whom notices should be sent, in what form, and how quickly.

Litigation. The possibilities for litigation against a company in crisis can seem endless. (At the end of this chapter, we discuss litigation that might be brought *by* the company in crisis.) There can be litigation from third parties (individuals or a class) who are directly affected by the crisis. Such actions can be based upon tort law or contract. Federal and/or state regulators or prosecutors can bring actions under various statutes and regulations. Those actions can be civil or criminal in nature. Shareholders can bring claims based upon breaches of fiduciary duties, violations of the securities laws, or both. Employees can bring a couple of different types of claims. An employee who was a whistleblower warning of the facts that led to the crisis may claim retaliation; there are quite a number of anti-retaliation laws. An employee who was fired because of actions that contributed to the crisis may claim that he or she is unfairly being held accountable.

So, who besides the company is the target of these actions? Directors and officers are the principal targets. When the claim is based on a breach of fiduciary duty, it is typically brought as a "derivative" suit. A derivative suit is litigation that is brought in the name of the corporation and is initiated by shareholders. If pursued and successful, any damages are recovered by the corporation; that recovery indirectly benefits the shareholders proportionately, because the value of the corporation itself is increased.

A derivative suit typically begins with a demand being made on the board to commence the litigation. The theory for this approach is that a decision to bring litigation on behalf of the company is like any other management decision and should be made by the board. When the demand is made, in most instances a special litigation committee is appointed to consider whether a claim should be brought. The committee must be populated by directors who are both independent and also disinterested in the outcome—that is, not potential targets of the suit. The committee will then retain independent counsel to guide them through the process and investigate the allegations. The committee might conclude that the allegations have no merit and determine not to pursue the suit. Even if the allegations are found to have merit, the committee may conclude not to pursue the litigation on the basis of the kinds of factors that would lead a board not to pursue litigation against any third party—for example, the expected cost of litigation will exceed the potential recoveries on a risk-adjusted basis. Such a determination generally will be respected by a court, so long as it is satisfied that the committee was truly independent and disinterested and did a thorough job.

There are situations in which the demand on the board is "excused" because of "futility"—that is, there could not be a legitimate special litigation committee because all of the directors participated in the acts that allegedly constituted a breach of fiduciary duty. During the course of the litigation (which can take years), the makeup of the board can change—some of the defendant directors may leave and be replaced by new directors who are not defendants. In this situation, a special litigation committee comprising these new, independent, and disinterested directors can be appointed to decide whether the corporation should *continue* the litigation. The new committee can dismiss the pending case—even if it had been properly commenced by the shareholders—so long as:

- the decision to dismiss does not involve a breach of fiduciary duties; and
- the committee has concluded, "after an objective and thorough investigation," that the continuation of the suit would be "detrimental to the company" and that conclusion is not "wrongful."

However, because of the legitimacy of the commencement of the suit and because "directors are passing judgment on fellow directors," the courts impose a strict standard of review before agreeing to such a dismissal. "The corporation should have the burden of proving independence, good faith and a reasonable investigation," and then the "court should determine, applying its own independent business judgment, whether the motion should be granted."[3]

Regardless of the type of claim brought against a director or officer, there is likely to be an indemnification obligation on the part of the company to pay legal fees, and a related but independent obligation to advance expenses to be incurred by the individual. The specific obligation may require paying for separate counsel if there is a potential conflict between the interests of the company and the individual. In any event, it may be prudent to provide separate counsel for an employee (or, for a group of employees, "pool counsel") to encourage them to be truthful and forthcoming in any investigation.

Even before the formal commencement of litigation, when it is merely threatened, it is critical that the company take reasonable steps to preserve documents (including emails, texts, and other electronic forms) that could be pertinent to the case. This typically involves the issuance of a "document hold" notice. When such a notice, to be effective, must go out to a large number of employees and others, that fact will often influence a decision about the timing of a broader public disclosure if it hasn't already been made. At the same time, it would likely be prudent to notify the insurance companies that have written relevant policies, which may be those covering property and casualty, recalls, and director and officer liability.

When litigation is in the discovery phase or is going to trial, the question arises "who will be the company's witnesses?" Certainly, for maximum harassment value and to create settlement leverage, plaintiffs will sometimes seek to call the CEO. The company will, of course, want to offer up a lower-level executive. A court being asked by a defendant to issue a protective order to prevent the deposition of a CEO will apply the "apex witness doctrine." The court will need to decide if the alternative witness offered up by the company is sufficiently connected to the facts of the case. When the CEO is continually front and center on all communications and, through that, gives the impression of unique personal knowledge of the facts, it may not be possible to substitute another executive in the role of the witness. Regardless of whoever becomes a company witness, he or she must devote the time necessary to be exquisitely prepared. There are many defense counsel who will tell the same story—they schedule a full day for witness preparation, but when they sit down with a busy (and annoyed) CEO, senior officer, or director, they are told, after about an hour, "I've got this . . . no need for more."

Regulatory Proceedings. Regulatory proceedings against a company in crisis often result from the facts that lead to the crisis. While these matters are very similar to litigation, there is one big difference that is easy to overlook. A company's crisis can also be a crisis for its regulator. If, for example, a regulator has oversight jurisdiction about the safety of the company's goods or services, and there is a failure along those lines, the regulator can be in the crosshairs of Congress and/or the press right along with the company. This can certainly affect the demeanor and demands of the regulators and their reactions to a company's public statements. The best way to address the potential for dealing with regulators during a crisis is to have reasonably nonconfrontational—or even appropriately cordial—relationships before any crisis develops.

Internal Investigations. In a non-crisis context, internal investigations are most commonly triggered by allegations of wrongdoing targeting members of management. In the context of a crisis, investigations may be part of anticipating and defending litigation against the company. Or, they may be necessary to respond to a shareholder derivative demand to sue corporate fiduciaries. Or, they may be requested by regulatory agencies, with a request/requirement that the results thereof be shared with those agencies. (Yes, on occasion the agencies, including the SEC, will ask the company to do their investigative work for them.) Finally, as noted in Chapter 10, a root cause analysis has many of the attributes of an internal investigation.

Regardless of its genesis, there are some commonalities associated with any internal investigation. When there is a concern about a management conflict, the internal investigation is often run under the direction of a committee of independent directors, who retain independent counsel. Similarly, if the investigation is in response to a pending derivative suit demand, it will be run by a special litigation committee (SLC) comprising directors who will be able to withstand heightened scrutiny of their independence. As noted in Chapter 4, this heightened scrutiny is illustrated by a number of Delaware cases that have considered whether business, charitable, and (even) social relationships between SLC members and the directors and officers they are passing judgment on would render the SLC members unable to perform their tasks in a dispassionate manner.[4]

Another commonality is that counsel conducting the investigation must make clear to the employees they will inevitably be interviewing that they (the counsel) represent the company, not any individual employee. This is done by giving the employee an "Upjohn warning" (sometimes referred to as a "corporate Miranda"). A short version of this is "We have been retained by the [company] [board of directors] to investigate _____. What you and others tell us will enable us to provide advice to the [company] [board]. Our interview with you is confidential and protected by the attorney-client privilege. The [company] [board] will not tolerate any reprisals against you and is asking you to cooperate with this investigation. But, to be clear, our client is the [company] [board], so if the [company] [board] chooses to disclose to others what you tell us or to waive the privilege, it can do so without your consent or telling you. If you would feel more comfortable being represented by counsel when speaking with us, you are certainly free to hire a lawyer of your own. In the meantime, it is important that you understand that you keep what we discuss confidential—including not sharing any of what we discuss with others who we might be interviewing. Do you agree?" Despite the somewhat scary message, if delivered with tact, this usually does not lead a recipient to clam up. An employee who refuses to cooperate may face termination of employment. A former employee may be breaching a requirement to co-operate contained in a severance agreement if he or she fails to do so.

While a "mulligan" may be fine in a friendly game of golf, a "do-over" of an internal investigation can be expensive and adversely impact repu-tation. For example, eight months after McDonald's fired its CEO, Steve Easterbrook, for having an inappropriate relationship with a subordinate, and paid him a $40 million package, it sued him to recoup compensa-tion. The company claimed that Easterbrook lied and concealed evidence about another inappropriate relationship. As reported in the press, the lawsuit "raises . . . questions . . . about how diligent [the company] was in looking into Mr. Easterbrook's conduct before dismissing him with a generous compensation package . . . the initial review did not include a thorough search of the executive's email account."[5] And in the following annual shareholders meeting, the chair of the McDonald's compensation committee was targeted by shareholders in a "withhold" vote campaign. Similarly, questions were raised in a shareholder derivative demand about the thoroughness of a first investigation into the Jeffrey Epstein relation-ship involving L Brands/Victoria's Secret, as well as the independence of counsel. Those questions resulted in a second investigation.

Settlements. Litigation and regulatory proceedings can often be re-solved through settlements. Settlements can take place before a trial or administrative proceeding, or afterward and during the appeal process. Those settlements can come in a variety of forms.

First of all, there is the matter of compensation to the victims of the underlying facts that led to the crisis. When compensation is to be paid in cash, the two big areas of negotiation are obvious—how much and when? "How much" can be a discussion about restitution, and also punishment. "When" relates to whether the amounts are to be paid out over time. There is a third issue that is relevant to negotiations—where is the cash to come from? When the answer to that question includes insurers—primary and other layers—things can get complicated. The company will need to un-derstand that the insurers will likely want to participate in the negotia-tions and will seek some element of reimbursement in the form of future premium increases.

Of course, not all compensation needs to be in the form of cash. Settle-ments of class actions can involve coupons or other forms of trade credit. Often the "headline" number in the settlement includes the face amount of such credits, despite the fact that they will never be realized by the plaintiffs. Finally, in an extreme case, such as when the defendant has filed for bankruptcy, the negotiation includes a discussion of how much of the post-bankruptcy company the plaintiff class will own.

Then there is the annoying question of the fees to be paid to the attorneys who represent the class of victims.

If the settlement involves addressing criminal charges, in addition to cash fines, there are three major varieties of settlement. In order of least to most desirable from the company's standpoint, they are: a guilty plea, a plea of nolo contendere, no indictment but a deferred prosecution agreement (DPA), or a non-prosecution agreement (NPA). The negotiations about these alternatives significantly involve a discussion of so-called "collateral consequences." That is, aside from the shareholders, will other stakeholders (e.g., employees, suppliers, creditors, and communities) bear the brunt of the resolution of the case? Is an indictment or a guilty plea the equivalent of the death penalty for the company? Consider the effect of the indictment of Arthur Andersen because of its involvement with Enron. AA was seriously damaged by the indictment alone and was put out of business when it was convicted of obstruction of justice. The reversal of that conviction by the US Supreme Court came too late to save the firm, and the entire public accounting profession was dramatically impacted.

Under some circumstances, there is the potential for criminal charges against individuals. In the years following the 2008 Global Financial Crisis, there was a frequent refrain from politicians and others lamenting the fact that no individuals had been carted off to jail. The Department of Justice responded with the "Yates memo" in 2015 during the closing years of the Obama administration. That memo was seemingly designed to encourage individual US Attorneys to pursue accountability for individuals when their companies were settling criminal proceedings.[6] While that position was walked back a bit under the Trump DOJ, it was not completely repealed.[7]

A settlement can also involve requirements about future conduct. A company may be required to enter into a so-called "corporate integrity agreement" (with the amusing acronym of CIA). Such agreements can contain a variety of undertakings—hiring a consultant to investigate and report to regulators on areas of activity that pertain to the events that caused the crisis, establishing a compliance committee of the board, and/or hiring a "monitor" to oversee the activities of the company for some period of time and to make reports to a prosecutor, regulator, and/or the public.

Companies that have had to accept monitorships are frequently stunned by the cost and operational disruption associated with having a monitor. In 2018, the US Department of Justice issued a memorandum to its criminal division personnel entitled "Selection of Monitors in Criminal Division Matters." The memo was viewed as giving companies a greater opportunity to avoid a monitorship. Among the factors set forth in the memo as relevant to requiring a monitor are "whether the corporation has made . . . improvements to its corporate compliance programs," and whether "misconduct occurred under different corporate leadership or within a compliance environment that no longer exists within a company."[8] Note the encouragement of a management change embedded in the phrase "different corporate leadership." Then, in October 2021, the Department of Justice announced in a speech by the Deputy Attorney General that "to the extent that prior Justice Department guidance suggested that monitorships are disfavored or are the exception, I am rescinding that guidance."[9]

Finally, a settlement with individuals can involve fines, termination of employment, and (in a regulated industry) a bar for some period of time, or even for life, from being involved with companies in that industry.[10]

Duration of Proceedings. One reality of crisis-related litigation is that it can persist long, long after the events that created the crisis have ended. Crisis management is more of a marathon (or ultra-marathon) than a sprint. This is especially true of crises that fall into Category #1. And this observation applies to both the company and individuals.

Set forth below are timelines for five different corporate crises. These timelines illustrate several things: the multiple types of litigation and regulatory matters that crisis managers must address, the fact that settling all matters at once through a "global settlement" may not be possible, and the protracted duration of the legal aspects of crises.

BP Deepwater Horizon Explosion and Oil Spill. As this timeline shows, the legal aspects of the disaster continued five years after the explosion and two years after the completion of the cleanup efforts. The legal proceedings ultimately cost BP approximately $65 billion.

- April 2010—Explosion kills 11 workers on the offshore oil platform and ultimately releases some 5 million barrels of oil into the Gulf of Mexico.
- April through June 2010—Multiple governmental investigations begin and lawsuits are filed.
- May 2010—BP CEO Tony Hayward, in a comment to the press meant to convey a corporate apology, utters the phrase "I want to get my life back."
- June 2010—Oil begins washing up on Gulf Coast beaches.
- July 2010—Well is capped.

- August 2010—Well is declared to be in a "static condition."
- October 2010—Hayward is replaced as CEO.
- 2011—National Commission report is issued and Congressional hearings take place.
- 2012—Criminal case against the company settles with $4.5 billion in fines; three company individuals are charged criminally; civil class action settles without a limitation on costs to be incurred by BP (but an estimate of $7.8 billion in payments to be made).
- 2013—Coastal cleanup is completed.
- 2014—Company is found grossly negligent in a civil case brought by federal and state governments.
- 2015—The governmental civil suit settles for $18.7 billion; one of the charged executives is acquitted, and criminal charges against the other two are dropped by the government.

Takata Airbags. The first of 16 fatalities due to the defective airbags occurred in 2009. The legal aspects of the crisis ended nine years later with the completion of the Takata bankruptcy proceeding. This timeline does not include the spillover to Takata's customers that had to deal with the claims brought against them.

- 2002–2015—Takata airbags are manufactured and sold to car and truck manufacturers for installation in new vehicles.
- 2008—First recall.
- 2009—First report of a fatality.
- 2014—First class-action lawsuit is filed.
- 2014—*New York Times* reports that executives were aware of defects as early as 2004.
- 2015—Company is fined $14,000 per day for failure to cooperate with the National Highway Traffic Safety Administration (NHTSA); NHTSA imposes a $200 million civil penalty and a monitor is appointed; three executives are fired.
- 2017—Company pleads guilty to deceiving automakers and reaches a $1 billion settlement with DOJ; company files bankruptcy and is sold to a Chinese manufacturer; fired executives are indicted and plead guilty.
- 2018—Bankruptcy judge approves trust fund for victims.
- 2019—New recalls of airbags due to a different defect!

Volkswagen "Dieselgate." The actions of the company that led to the crisis took place for five years before they were discovered. After discovery, the legal aspects continued for seven years . . . and counting.

- 2009–2015—The company deploys software to activate emission controls only during lab testing.
- 2014—Discrepancies are discovered between emissions results in road tests and lab tests; regulators begin investigations; stock price falls; CEO Martin Winterkorn resigns.
- 2017—The company pleads guilty to criminal charges and pays a $2.8 billion fine.
- 2018—Former CEO Winterkorn is criminally charged in the United States.
- 2019—Winterkorn is criminally charged in Germany; SEC files suit against the company and Winterkorn for securities fraud in the sale of bonds and asset-backed securities (ABS) from 2014 to 2015.
- 2021—Winterkorn and other executives pay $351 million to settle civil lawsuits. Criminal charges continue.

Blue Bell Creameries Listeria Outbreak. The crisis was the result of a listeria outbreak in 2015, although the seeds of the crisis were planted years before that. The legal aspects of the crisis took six years to play out.

- 2009–2013—Regulators find compliance failures.
- 2013–2014—Listeria is found in the company's plants.
- 2015—An outbreak of listeria in the company's products causes 3 deaths; a limited recall is followed by a full recall.
- 2015–2016—The company obtains equity funding on an emergency basis.
- 2017—Delaware lawsuit is filed by shareholders, alleging breach of fiduciary duties.
- 2019—Delaware Supreme Court decides for the shareholders.
- 2020—The company pleads guilty to misdemeanor criminal charges and the company is fined $17.25 million by the DOJ; felony charges against the CEO are dropped over a technicality.

Wells Fargo Fraudulent Accounts. From the date the fraudulent accounts scheme first surfaced in a newspaper article until the resolution of the last remaining legal matter was seven years.

- 2011–2016—Approximately 1.5 million unauthorized deposit accounts and 0.5 million credit card accounts are created; upon discovery, the bank fires 5,300 employees.
- 2013—*LA Times* article first reveals the issue.
- 2016—CEO John Stumpf testifies in Senate hearings, then resigns and is replaced by Tim Sloan; the bank settles with Consumer

Financial Protection Bureau (CFPB), Office of the Comptroller of the Currency (OCC), and city attorney of LA with $185 million in fines; the bank settles the customer class action for $142 million.

- 2017—Press reports that more than 0.8 million borrowers for auto loans were charged for unneeded auto insurance between 2012 and 2016. Former employee is awarded $5.4 million and ordered reinstated by OSHA in whistleblower case.
- 2018—The bank settles the shareholder class action for $480 million; the bank settles claims by 50 states' attorneys general for $575 million. The bank agrees to a Consent Order with the Comptroller of the Currency relating to a "compliance risk management program that constituted reckless[,] unsafe or unsound practices." Among other things, the bank agrees to appoint a "Compliance Committee of at least three (3) members," including a majority independent directors.
- 2019—CEO Sloan resigns.
- 2020—The bank settles with the US DOJ for $3.0 billion and agrees to a deferred prosecution agreement; former CEO Stumpf agrees with the DOJ to a $17.5 million fine and is barred from the industry for life and three other executives are fined by the OCC; finally, CEO Stumpf agrees with the SEC to a $2.5 million fine.
- 2021—The Comptroller of the Currency fines the bank $250 million for failing to comply adequately with the 2018 Consent Order. Senator Elizabeth Warren asks the Federal Reserve to force a separation of the bank's commercial and investment banking operations, asserting that the bank has a "broken culture."

Claims to Be Brought by the Company in Crisis. Not all crisis-associated litigation is brought against the company in crisis. The company may have claims against others. Most obviously, this would be the case in a Category #3 crisis. But it may also be the case in a Category #1 or Category #2 crisis (if claims against the company arise because of a culpable employee). Claims against third parties should be analyzed thoroughly and in a timely fashion. If such claims can only be considered after more facts develop and that appropriate delay is causing concerns about statutes of limitations, the company should seek and obtain a "tolling agreement" from the third party or parties. Such an agreement effectively hits the "pause button" on the statute of limitations clock.

Another claim that a company might bring and that should at least be considered is a compensation "clawback" claim. If the crisis causes or is otherwise associated with an accounting restatement, a clawback claim could be mandated by the provisions of either Sarbanes-Oxley[11] or Dodd-

Frank.[12] Or there may be contractual based clawbacks under executive employment agreements or under severance policies. As discussed in Chapter 2, one of the more interesting policies along these lines is that of Goldman Sachs. A clawback under that policy is triggered by an executive's "failure to appropriately consider risk." If the events that trigger a clawback claim of any kind rise to the level of a breach of fiduciary duty, it may be the case that the exposure of the executives is not limited to the amount of the compensation to be clawed back. It is possible that the executives would ask the company to waive any other claims in return for settling a dispute over a clawback. Depending on the facts, the independent and disinterested members of a board, with the benefit of advice of counsel, might agree to do so. However, they should consider such a request very carefully before agreeing to such a waiver.

Another category of claims by the company in crisis that should be investigated and preserved is claims against insurance carriers. Depending upon the type of crisis, any number of types of policies might respond to the company's losses. Step one to preserving the claim is to make a timely notice as required under the policies. Step two is to be sure to appropriately involve the insurers in settlement discussions with plaintiffs and co-defendants. Coverage claims against insurers are often somewhat esoteric and will require retaining specialized counsel.

Privilege Considerations. Because of all the litigation and regulatory issues described above that can arise in the context of any crisis, it is important that legal privilege be preserved as much as possible and waived only in a thoughtful manner. This involves considering such things as who counsel is engaged by, who retains the non-lawyer consultants, who receives communications from counsel (or even participates in meetings with counsel), what is the form of any report of an internal investigation and, if it needs to be communicated to a regulator (or even prosecutor), how is that done and what steps are to be taken to prevent accidental disclosure of confidential and/or privileged documents. Sensitivity to privilege issues is especially important in the preparation of all types of communications. For this reason alone, it is critical that the lawyers and the communications professionals have a close and collaborative working relationship. Even after taking all of the precautions possible, it is wise to exercise care and discretion in the creation of documents. Not all precautions work all of the time, and in the context of a crisis there is a risk that the "crime/fraud exception" will apply.

7

What Do We Say?
Communications Aspects

Leaders in crisis function as many things. They are primary givers of information, so they have to know the facts. They must master the data. Are they managerially competent? Most of all, are they trustworthy and credible. Or do people sense that they are spinning, finagling, covering up failures or shading the facts. It is in crisis that you see the difference between showmanship and leadership.

PEGGY NOONAN, *Wall Street Journal*, February 29–March 1, 2020

In any crisis, you will almost certainly be second-guessed on everything you do, but especially on how you communicate. Your board, senior staff, employees, lawyers, trustees, influential alumni, regulators, elected officials, customers, investors, suppliers, beat reporters, TV talking heads, issue-specific activists, and social media trolls will have opinions about everything. What should you have said? How did you say it? And to whom? Bad news travels amazingly fast and people are drawn to it. Slow responses are always heavily criticized.

Another challenge is that there is no shortage of conventional wisdom about communicating in a crisis. "Get out there." "Show you are in control." "Don't speculate." "Demonstrate concern." "Keep the stakeholders informed." "Feed the media." "Be transparent." "Avoid attempts at humor." "Get ahead of the bad news." The problem is that almost everyone has heard these maxims, but they have little or no practical experience in what they mean and how to implement them in a live, fast-moving situation where the facts and situational circumstances are not always completely clear.

In this chapter, we will summarize some of the key lessons from some of the best books on crisis communications on what to say and to whom in a crisis (see Appendix B for further reading). We will also add, from our own many years of working across different crises, thoughts on how to apply the lessons in real time.

Concentric Circles:[1]
Aligning Around Causes, Fixes, Next Steps, and the Message

Figuring out what to say in a crisis is not usually that complicated. While often easier said than done, for starters, you just need to have your head about you and move fast, quickly aligning around a solid, common understanding about what needs to be done, not just what needs to be said.

If you know what must be done to solve a crisis—or at least decide on the initial action steps—you often have the core of the message. All of your audiences want, at the most basic level, to know what happened, how it affects them, what you are going to do to fix the problem, and how you intend to regain trust and get back to normal. Of course, any true crisis presents threats to reputation, normal operations, and business continuity. And crises often result in necessary, sometimes far-reaching change—in behavior, operations, and sometimes leadership.

We have found it useful when advising companies and institutions in crisis to think in terms of concentric circles of key audiences as an organizing principle for deciding on and executing a communications plan in a crisis. The innermost circle of people making initial decisions should have good knowledge of the organization's constituents, be able to get information on what happened, and be able to frame a view on what actions are going to be taken.

A typical set of concentric circles will begin with the innermost circle of senior-most executives—at least 4–5 people who are empowered to make decisions and who have the right qualities and expertise to manage a crisis. From there, direct reports would typically be in the next ring. They are often best positioned to provide knowledgeable perspectives on the viability of the action plan and resonance of the messaging. If they buy fully into the "inner circle" plan, execution will be better, and they will be stronger ambassadors for the message.

"Inner circles" are best identified in advance and usually represent critical company functions (HR, legal, finance, IR, government affairs, and communications), business unit leaders, and subject matter experts (IT—especially in a cyber incident—engineering, production, logistics, security, etc.). In most cases, it is helpful to add experienced, trusted heads (aka "gray hairs") from the outside to lend perspective, challenge assumptions, and ask tough questions. This inner circle will need to make judgments in real time— judgments that lead to concrete actions, including, as discussed in Chapter 6, legally required disclosures—an 8-K, a regulatory filing, a press release, and so on.

Beyond legally required communications, which help set a framework for broader communications, you will need to assess what else to say to convince your key constituents that you have control of a crisis—or that you are working to get control.

Every organization can without much difficulty prioritize its constituents into a set of concentric circles around the inner circle of senior leadership. See sample illustration below. Once you have done that, deciding what each group needs to know, what they want to hear, and the questions they want answered becomes much easier.

The next ring is often a board of directors or trustees who will—if they are good—ask tough questions and be sensitive to outside concerns. Board reaction is critical because it is really the best way to get a read on external reaction to a message before it goes external.

Because convening a board is usually difficult with short notice, you will usually want to keep a chairman, a lead director, or one or two of your most influential board members in the loop—sometimes in the inner circle or just beyond.

Given tight time frames in a crisis, this series of verbal communications—at least in the "inner circle"—should be had no more than one to two hours from initial awareness of a crisis or potential crisis. This may seem short, but harsh opinions form quickly, and being seen to be on top of things immediately—even when you can say little, for example, in a crash or accident that has caused loss of life—can buy you time to get organized. More on this below.

Once you have informed and received feedback from your board or appropriate lead directors, your messaging moves to the next ring—usually internal and encompassing union leaders, employees, works councils, and so on. While these are generally considered internal audiences, they are effectively public communications and must be treated as such. Especially in larger organizations, you should assume that any communication to employees will find its way to investors (including employee stockholders) and media. However you prioritize audiences in a specific circumstance, all of the outer rings—regulators, investors, customers, suppliers, vendors, and media—need to be addressed in ways that speak to their specific questions and concerns.

The concentric circles have another purpose as well. In looking at the circles, consider the impact and influence each ring has on the rings beyond it, and the feedback loops that they create. For example, if your innermost ring of senior-most executives is in disarray and lands on messaging that appears defensive, overly legalistic, or tone deaf, there is no way that it will fly with the next ring, and the ring after that, and so on. The outer rings will quickly lose confidence in the management of the message and you will lose control of your crisis.

If your response is solid and investors and analysts believe management

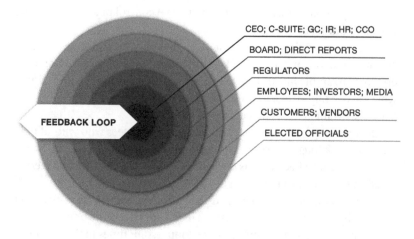

is doing a good job, that will be reflected in the media. If regulators are satisfied, that will be reflected in the media. If employees are positive about the steps their management team is taking, that will be reflected in the press too. All constituents talk to each other in one way or another, and understanding this ecosystem is key to a good communications strategy.

While you do need to be prepared to manage press interest early in a crisis—and failing to anticipate and address their immediate needs quickly can undermine perceptions that you have taken—or are taking—control of events—we often put them in the outer rings. This doesn't mean the press is not a critical constituency. Just the opposite. But relying on the press to carry your message unfiltered is a mistake. The press has agendas and, while there are many good, responsible journalists, the press is a decidedly imperfect channel to your most important direct constituencies.

Years ago, "the media" was almost your only option for rapid dissemination of critical information. Today, technology—including websites, social media, and video posts—can reach your targeted constituencies quickly and effectively, and your core audiences expect to hear from you in real time—not just through statements to the media. If your core stakeholders understand the story and believe you are doing the right thing, they will help you get your message out. Their comments to reporters can be helpful in mitigating negative press articles. But be mindful, however, that if you lose credibility by being less transparent than they expect, you will lose trust, and that could feed a negatively biased press and make it worse. Consistent with the mutually reinforcing mechanism of the circles, positive press reinforces management's messaging and this in turn increases constituent comfort levels. (See below, "Managing the Media.")

The Quality of Inner-Circle Conversations

The quality of conversations that take place in that inner-circle group of leaders and managers—in both anticipating what could go wrong and how to respond when something does go wrong—is probably the main determinant of whether a crisis will be managed successfully.

If your messaging does not fully address the concerns of an engaged and empowered inner circle, it is unlikely to satisfy the concerns of those who are not in the decision-making loop, and further out in the concentric circles.

So how does this work in real life? Let's start with the quality of the initial conversation. The inner circle in crisis management should represent the constituencies who impact a company's ability to survive a crisis successfully: employees through HR, legal, perhaps IT, government affairs, investor relations, communications or external affairs, operations, business-specific leaders, and subject matter experts. The executives working in these areas, when engaged, can on any given day usually list the 5–10 things that keep them up at night. In a crisis, the list is likely to be more acute.

It is worth noting that of all the functions—with the exception of the CEO—chief communications officers will often have the widest lens through which to view the competing interests of all the impacted constituencies. They can often see and articulate the impact of an action or public statement in one part of the organization on other stakeholders. And the best are adept and courageous enough to conduct "red-face tests" of proposed actions or statements before they go public.

Prior to a crisis, management teams should meet regularly to share and update these lists. The most significant issues should be planned for. Basic protocols for what would be done in each situation should be considered. And mitigating steps or initiatives should be prioritized, ahead of any crisis. Some companies routinely do tabletop exercises, including complex injects and role play, sometimes extending over days.

While communications materials will always need to be adapted to a specific situation, being ready with a core package can save critical hours and position you if need be to move quickly. Among the most useful documents is a core holding statement that can be issued to press and other stakeholders as you assess a specific situation. It will generally acknowledge that an issue exists—what and where—and say broadly what you know and what you are doing to learn more. It will refer to your commitment as appropriate to update stakeholders, and it will underscore your cultural values and commitment to set things right. The best statements are short, concise, and written to be included in their entirety in quickly drawn-up press reports. Below are just a few examples:

> Target Holding Statement, December 19, 2013: Payment Card Data Breach:[2]
> "Target today confirmed it is aware of unauthorized access to payment card data that may have impacted certain guests making credit and debit card purchases in its U.S. stores. Target is working closely with law enforcement and financial institutions and has identified and resolved the issue. Target's first priority is preserving the trust of our guests and we have moved swiftly to address this issue, so guests can shop with confidence. We regret any inconvenience this may cause," said Gregg Steinhafel, chairman, president, and chief executive officer, Target. "We take this matter very seriously and are working with law enforcement to bring those responsible to justice. Approximately 40 million credit and debit card accounts may have been impacted between Nov. 27 and Dec. 15, 2013. Target alerted authorities and financial institutions immediately after it was made aware of the unauthorized access and is putting all appropriate resources behind these efforts. Among other actions, Target is partnering with a leading third-party forensics firm to conduct a thorough investigation of the incident."
> Apple Holding Statement after iCloud theft of celebrity photos in 2014:[3]
> "We wanted to provide an update to our investigation into the theft of photos of certain celebrities. When we learned of the theft, we were outraged and immediately mobilized Apple's engineers to discover the source. Our customers' privacy and security are of utmost importance to us. After more than 40 hours of investigation, we have discovered that certain celebrity accounts were compromised by a very targeted attack on usernames, passwords and security questions, a practice that has become all too common on the Internet. None of the cases we have investigated has resulted from any breach in any of Apple's systems including iCloud® or Find my iPhone. We are continuing to work with law enforcement to help identify the criminals involved. To protect against this type of attack, we advise all users to always use a strong password and enable two-step verification. Both of these are addressed on our website at http://support.apple.com/kb/ht4232."
> Facebook and Cambridge Analytica, 2018:[4]
> Mark Zuckerberg's post on Facebook: "I want to share an update on the Cambridge Analytica situation—including the steps we've

already taken and our next steps to address this important issue. We have a responsibility to protect your data, and if we can't then we don't deserve to serve you. I've been working to understand exactly what happened and how to make sure this doesn't happen again. The good news is that the most important actions to prevent this from happening again today we have already taken years ago. But we also made mistakes, there's more to do, and we need to step up and do it."

Samsung Galaxy Note 7 phone fires, 2016:[5]

"Samsung is committed to producing the highest quality products and we take every incident report from our valued customers very seriously. In response to recently reported cases of the new Galaxy Note 7, we conducted a thorough investigation and found a battery cell issue. To date (as of September 1) there have been 35 cases that have been reported globally and we are currently conducting a thorough inspection with our suppliers to identify possible affected batteries in the market.

"However, because our customers' safety is an absolute priority at Samsung, we have stopped sales of the Galaxy Note 7. For customers who already have Galaxy Note 7 devices, we will voluntarily replace their current device with a new one over the coming weeks. Instructions on the replacement process will be shared next week.

"We acknowledge the inconvenience this may cause in the market, but this is to ensure that Samsung continues to deliver the highest quality products to our customers. We are working closely with our partners to ensure the replacement experience is as convenient and efficient as possible."

Johnson & Johnson talc in baby powder, response to Reuters article, 2018:[6]

"The Reuters article is one-sided, false and inflammatory. Johnson & Johnson's baby powder is safe and asbestos-free. Studies of more than 100,000 men and women show that talc does not cause cancer or asbestos-related disease. Thousands of independent tests by regulators and the world's leading labs prove our baby powder has never contained asbestos. J&J attorneys provided Reuters with hundreds of documents and directly responded to dozens of questions in order to correct misinformation and falsehoods. Notwithstanding this, Reuters repeatedly refused to meet with our representatives to review the facts and refused to incorporate much of the material we provided them.

"The Reuters article is wrong in three key areas:

"The article ignores that thousands of tests by J&J, regulators, leading independent labs, and academic institutions have repeatedly shown that our talc does not contain asbestos.

"The article ignores that J&J has cooperated fully and openly with the U.S. FDA and other global regulators, providing them with all the information they requested over decades. We have also made our cosmetic talc mines and processed talc available to regulators for testing. Regulators have tested both, and they have always found our talc to be asbestos-free.

"The article ignores that J&J has always used the most advanced testing methods available to confirm that our cosmetic talc does not contain asbestos. Every method available to test J&J's talc for asbestos has been used by J&J, regulators, or independent experts, and all of these methods have all found that our cosmetic talc is asbestos-free.

"Johnson & Johnson will continue to defend the safety of our product. For the truth and facts about talc, please go to www.factsabout talc.com."

* * *

During an actual crisis, at least some in the inner circle will have a strong view on what led to the problem. They should be able to candidly assess decisions, events, and failings that should have been examined more closely. The best organizations identify these risks and are already looking at potential mitigation before a problem happens.

Keep in mind that failing to recognize and address a known weakness (especially when identified by whistleblowers or in emails/instant messages in legal discovery) is one of the first things you will be criticized for in a crisis, and one of the most difficult things to recover from.

When a crisis does occur, communications become easier once the inner circle agrees about the course of action. The people who are impacted want to know what happened, why you think it happened, and what you are going to do about it. If you don't have such alignment, your crisis management and crisis communications efforts are doomed.

In a major situation where lives are at risk, it is important also to separate "emergency response" from "crisis management." You will need to be in touch with what is happening on the ground and let the first responders do their thing, while the executive team focuses their own attention on scenarios, assessment of impact on the enterprise, required and tactical communications, recovery strategies, and so on.

Boeing's extraordinarily complex 737 MAX crisis, of course, will provide many lessons on crisis management and communications for years to come. Even after the March 2019 crash of Ethiopian Airlines flight 302, five months after Lion Air flight 610 went down off the coast of Indonesia in 2018, the notion that engineering assumptions underlying the MCAS software had contributed in a significant way to the crash was anathema to many at a very proud Boeing organization. Incorrect and outdated assumptions about what pilots should have been able to do, an overly legalistic and engineering driven response, and a US-centric view of a rapidly expanding global aviation ecosystem blinded much of a well-intentioned Boeing leadership team and most outside observers to the realities of their situation and marketplace.

In hindsight, it seems clear that confusion in the inner circle about what happened and why, right after the Lion Air crash, compounded the crisis. And reassurances from the siloed engineering side of the house appeared to lull much of the rest of the organization into some complacency about how it should respond. Much of the organization fixated on the software solution and a quick return to normal. Too little focus was given—at least in the early days—to victim impact and the core assumptions that had been made around training, the amount of information provided on new software in the aircraft, and how pilots would handle abnormal situations in the relatively new airplane. There were also communications constraints imposed by international regulations, and some very real and justified concerns around the level of experience and quality of pilot training and maintenance procedures at the two airlines whose planes crashed. Also, it turned out that Boeing may have been too quick to assume that all of its engineers on the MAX program were interacting in good faith with regulators—as email evidence ultimately suggested. This led to the $2.5 billion criminal settlement with DOJ, and Boeing has had to work hard to repair trust with US and overseas regulators. It also had to take steps to improve relationships with supply chain partners.

Especially following the second crash in March 2019, many observers inside and outside of Boeing were calling for Boeing's CEO and others to "get out there" and tell the Boeing story. The problem was that, in the initial phases of the crisis, the story Boeing wanted to tell was not convincing, and it was again constrained by international rules on what it could say before independent investigators did their reports.

Most at the senior levels of the company predicted a quick return to service after grounding—a view that persisted well into 2019. Unfortunately—as it unfolded—it became clear that a much bigger picture had been missed. It dawned too slowly for everyone across the entire Boeing organization that these tragic crashes would dramatically reshape Boeing's reputation for product quality and safety, and would ultimately lead to a rethink of the global aviation ecosystem. As it turned out, the rethink became even more complicated due to the global COVID-19 Pandemic, which crushed demand for new aircraft for Boeing's commercial airliner customers.

Managing the Media

As noted above, the mistake many people make in crisis management is thinking that media is the primary channel for communicating to their constituencies.

Ultimately, in a crisis, your constituents want to hear directly from you—not through the media. If they hear from you live, over the phone, and through letters, emails, videos, and website and social media posts— and they believe you are telling a credible story—they will generally discount negative articles. If they don't believe you're telling the whole truth, they will gravitate to other sources. Your constituents' expectation is that you will manage media interest, not that it will be their primary source for information. You should always strive to be the most trusted source for news about your situation.

With the media, you are relying on someone else to tell your story. Even the best reporters who are impeccably sourced, knowledgeable, and willing to invest in building relationships with senior communications people and executives will quote unhelpful critics and others—from anonymous competitors and uninformed politicians to short sellers and activists—who may have agendas adverse to yours. While you want "balance," reporters are understandably wary of being accused of writing puff pieces or failing to be brutally objective about a given situation.

These days, unfortunately, you will more likely deal with inexperienced and ill-informed reporters who aren't likely to stay in the business long enough to care about building trusted relationships. They are often pressured to sensationalize articles to "capture eyeballs" and drive revenues. These types of reporters and those who specialize in generating "clickbait" with misleading headlines and "gotcha" stories that push an agenda rather than a balanced narrative make the media channel difficult, time consuming, and sometimes dangerous to manage. Frequently, it also makes it hard for communications staff to recommend executive engagement.

But tend the media you must. That does not mean you have to give them everything they want—just that you need to assess what's in your best interests, even if the relationship is, or becomes, mutually suspicious and contentious. Hearing what reporters have to say and the questions they ask can be valuable and may help inform your direct messaging to your core audiences.

Whatever the situation, however, basic principles in media management always apply, even with reporters you consider to be friendly. Agree to the ground rules for any conversation—beforehand. Have a common understanding about "off the record," "background," "deep background," and the various permutations.

"Off the record" is generally understood to be a conversation that cannot be used publicly in print. Some journalists will allow such conversations when there is a trusted relationship, so they can get guidance and context that they would not otherwise get. Other reporters don't agree to "off the record" conversations at all. Many of them discover, however, that their best sources and advocates dry up as a result, and they become less nuanced in their coverage. Unfortunately, in either case, information given "off the record" almost always finds its way into the public arena. Use only with extreme caution and don't start talking until you have agreement and are confident you can trust the reporter's word.

"Background" means what you say can be used but the attribution, if one is necessary, can be negotiated. For instance, "according to a person familiar with the situation." "Deep background" usually means the information can be used but that there will be no quotes or attributions at all.

Tell the truth but don't say more than you must. Stay on message. Do not speculate beyond your headlights. And always, always, always reiterate and confirm agreement on ground rules before you start talking.

Press conference calls and live press conferences are an efficient tool in a fast-moving situation but obviously come with significant risk. It is critical to prepare thoroughly for these—as much if not more than you would for an analyst earnings call.

Every company should have a peacetime media engagement strategy and relationships they can lean on in a crisis. It will be useful to have built such relationships when a crisis does hit.

Two more cautions. At the beginning of any crisis, reporters will try hard to persuade you to give them the inside track on information flow. Do not ever take at face value a reporter's promise to "help you tell your story." That will happen a lot, but the assumption that a reporter will indeed "help" or be an ally is usually misguided. Not always, but most always. Be extremely cautious. Even "off the record" information has come back to haunt many executives. Reporters will always try to find ways to use information they find interesting.

You will need to weigh the reporter relationship and whether your "help" to a given reporter is giving oxygen to a negative story and keeping your problem in the public eye. To avoid this, try to control the cadence and timing of news to the extent possible. More press around a crisis is not better.

Protecting Your CEO

While CEOs cannot be missing in action in a crisis, you should work to avoid overexposure, as it increases risk. And your lawyers will be sensitive to the bullseye it puts on your CEO's back for plaintiffs. (See the "apex witness" doctrine in Chapter 6.)

If you must go on television (general news programs most often best avoided), make sure you have prepped to crisply answer anticipated difficult questions. Never, ever, "wing it."

For CEOs these days, the picture is complicated by an aggressive anti-CEO social and political climate. Every crisis quickly becomes a referendum on the CEO, sometimes deservedly and many times not. A predictable, almost tribal drumbeat calling for the CEO's head quickly follows first news of many a crisis. Under this kind of pressure, a CEO can easily say the wrong thing. Consider BP's Tony Hayward's "I want my life back,"[7] Goldman's Lloyd Blankfein's "We're doing God's work,"[8] Boeing's Dennis Muilenburg's "There was no glitch,"[9] and United Airlines' well-intentioned but much-criticized statement issued by Oscar Munoz defending employees of contract carrier United Express when a passenger was dragged off one of their airplanes.

Protecting a CEO from a hostile crowd is a consideration in any crisis, and so is avoiding situations where he or she might say things that are unhelpful. Traditional PR advice (we will call it PR 101) has always been to "get your CEO out there." Increasingly, however, PR 201 suggests a more cautious approach—"But don't throw him or her to the wolves."

Being highly selective on saying yes to TV appearances and on-the-record interviews is smart and reasonable. Make sure you balance the pros and cons, and that you understand the format, leanings, and modus operandi of the reporters and producers. Be clear about ground rules. More than a few CEOs have assumed too much about what they can say in an "on the record" interview and not have it come back to haunt them. Consider Boeing CEO's David Calhoun when he vented on the record about his predecessor to a *New York Times* reporter,[10] resulting in a scathing article and a public apology.

Magazine-format television shows such as *60 Minutes* and *Dateline* are particularly dangerous vehicles for getting your message out in an unfiltered way, and normally best avoided. They are notorious for selective editing and camera angles to support an editorial bent and create drama their viewers expect. This doesn't mean that you always have to say no, but you must be extremely careful and have experienced advisors to assess the likelihood of a neutral to positive outcome. Most of the time, a simple statement to be read on air is best. It can't be edited, and the chances of a disastrous "hit piece" that can undermine a career are reduced.

When on-the-record interviews are difficult, consider continuing off-the-record and background engagement, where possible, to keep relationships warm and reporters reasonably constructive.

A CEO should be very aggressive in reaching out directly to core constituencies—speaking regularly to the board and working the phones, but also getting out of the office and walking the floor with employees, visiting personally with shareholders, and going to see customers. He or she should have a clear plan involving high personal touch with the people in the concentric circles.

Where it makes sense, he or she should also broaden the executive team empowered to do face-to-face diplomacy, reassurance, and information gathering. But remember, there is no real substitute for hearing directly and personally from the CEO.

Controlled venues, taped messages, and personal visits to employees, customers, and those impacted directly are all a vital part of the playbook today. While this doesn't always satisfy media, who will always want more—and your press relations people will want to please their contacts—it is much safer.

In the Boeing MAX crisis, there was considerable criticism by the media and many observers of CEO Dennis Muilenburg for not doing a lot of press. However, at the time of the crisis and even now in retrospect, there is nothing to suggest that having him do more press would have helped. In fact, just the opposite. But the sense that he was not "out there" was compounded by what appeared to be reticence to be more personally visible with a broader range of key constituencies.

Especially if there are victims, as in the Boeing situation, or in a plant or town where there has been an accident, it is important to show up quickly. Boeing's Muilenburg, while many who knew him understood he cared deeply about what had happened, was heavily criticized, and was taken to task at Congressional hearings for inexplicably failing to meet with the families of those who had died in the two crashes. In this case, meeting the families on their home turf in Indonesia and Ethiopia would have been a complicated "big lift," but many observers thought it clearly would have been worth the effort. By the time senior executives (but not the top brass) visited those countries, it was too little, too late.

In contrast, when a 1999 explosion at Ford's Rouge power plant in Dearborn, Michigan, killed 7 employees, Bill Ford and his wife visited the families of the deceased in their homes and one critically injured worker in the ICU. No media were informed, and there was no fanfare. It was just Henry Ford's great-grandson going to pay his personal respects to the people who worked for him. It was powerful and authentic, and the story filtered out to those who mattered.

Press Conferences

Press conferences can be extremely useful in very defined circumstances, but they are also fraught with peril if one is not well prepared for the questions and the group dynamic, which can take things into sometimes unanticipated directions.

In a fast-moving, high-profile situation, a live press conference can be an opportunity to show that you are in control of a situation and that you recognize the stakes. A live, well-managed appearance can be effective in presenting an unfiltered message, though derivative coverage will often incorporate analysis of what was said in both positive and negative ways.

The downsides of press conferences are that they can raise the profile of your crisis, be contentious, and put you on the firing line for reporters with agendas and "no win" questions that might have little to do with your specific crisis. For example, popular questions asked of CEOs in recent crises include: "Why don't you resign?" "Why aren't you in in jail?" "Will you give up your salary and other compensation while you work to resolve this crisis?" Reporters love to try to get a CEO to slip and say something that undermines the overall message.

The pros and cons of the press conference and the timing of one must be weighed carefully before exposing a CEO to this format. Significant attention to preparation is key. "Winging it" is always a mistake, and it is vital to test messaging and practice questions and answers with your team and external advisors before you take the podium.

CEOs are smart, confident, and extremely busy people. All too often, however, they bristle at the idea of media and press conference prep. Try not to take "no" or "I'll give you 30 minutes" for an answer. It takes a strong executive or advisor to insist on taking the time to go through the toughest questions—often predictable but sometimes out of left field. No person, no matter how smart or accomplished, does not get better with practice.

Consider Michael Bloomberg's failure to prepare for obvious attack lines in his first presidential campaign debate.[11] He almost certainly knew better, but by failing to prepare—can there be any other excuse under the circumstances?—he completely undermined himself and never recovered despite spending many millions on advertisements. This failure by someone so obviously smart and successful was a perfect example of the hubris that many CEOs evince around preparation.

Come up with the obvious and not-so-obvious questions and practice the answers—over and over. Tweak the answers and build on them. Practice "bridging" to your messages rather than sinking into a quagmire that feeds into your inquisitor's agenda.

As many lawyers will tell you, they run up against the same dynamic in deposition prep. The CEO shows up but, after 15 minutes, says, "I've got this" and exits the room. In depositions and press conferences, many defeats are snatched from the jaws of victory simply for failure to prepare. Do not do the same! Do not let your CEO do the same!

To Comment or No

Forever, "no comment" was the "go to" corner, preferred by lawyers everywhere, when a client is asked a difficult, potentially legally charged question. Over time, however, "no comment" began to be conflated in the minds of many media and the public with "nolo contendere"—a plea of no contest in which you decline to defend yourself and are presumed guilty, even if you don't formally admit it. It shouldn't be so—but it is.

Increasingly, "no comment" has evolved into "declined to comment," which has gained traction because it avoids the CEO or spokesperson being quoted as saying "no comment." A reporter has to report that you declined to comment rather than being able to quote you. A decline to comment is also interpreted to mean that a person is not yet ready to comment or defend, not that they can't defend—especially when caveated with "at this time." A reporter may simply report something like "a spokesperson declined to comment," or "the CEO declined to comment at this time," usually implying that a legal defense or statement will be forthcoming. This is nuance, of course, but an important one.

The art of not commenting continues to evolve—including with more elaborate statements of principle and commitment, which are needed to buy time—and it has often been lampooned—perhaps most famously in the BBC's dark dramatic comedy *House of Cards*—but is frequently necessary as you gather facts and prepare a coherent set of messages.

Privileged and Confidential; Rough Drafts

It is common practice for communications people to prepare notes and drafts as they work to an approved set of messaging that is ready for prime time. Often, as they begin to block out the messages, they don't have all the facts about an event and a legal strategy may not have been formulated. This creates risk.

A first line of defense is to ensure that the communications people are working at the direction of in-house or outside legal counsel. This allows you to label all materials prepared in anticipation of litigation as "Privileged and Confidential," which may prevent it from being discovered by a legal adversary. This kind of discovery can be problematic when an incautious communications person cooks up a document that is used to undermine final, approved arguments and messaging. The privileged and confidential designation at least allows attorneys to fight a de-designation, depending on the facts.

Until a document hold has been ordered—when destroying documents can result in prosecution—it is good housekeeping to regularly delete old drafts of communications materials. Arguments always evolve, and key facts are researched that improve the accuracy of messaging. If documents are to be reviewed publicly in court, and by the newspapers if leaked, better to have only the latest, most polished versions available.

Social Media and "Going Viral"

As has been attributed to Mark Twain, "a lie can travel halfway several times around the world before the truth has put on its shoes."[12] That seems quaint in this age of social media when pictures, utterances, legal actions, accidents—pretty much everything these days—can find a worldwide audience in seconds. Impressions are formed, stakeholders and regulators are forced to react, and pundits and trolls are quick to pounce.

Social media is challenging in a crisis. It drives narratives, it is impressionistic, and critics are rarely constrained by the truth. Responding to critiques and inaccuracies in newspaper comment sections or on a critic's social media channel can inflame the situation and embolden the trolls.

The best way to engage on social media is to have your own well-established social media channels. With your own channels—Instagram, Twitter, LinkedIn, and Facebook, to name a few—you can put out an authoritative story and showcase progress in addressing the crisis. When information put out by others is provably false, your channels are the best place to address it. It takes time to build a peacetime audience for your own social channels—and significant effort to create relevant content that will help you grow an audience—but it is worthwhile for many companies.

The Apology

Apologies in corporate and institutional crisis, or in personal situations, have been much written about, and some observers try to make them out to be more complex than they are. Good apologies work when rare, appropriate, and when they reflect common sense. We have all been the recipient of personal apologies on all ends of the spectrum, from the "I'm sorry you felt that way . . ." to a heartfelt expression of true remorse.

In short, good apologies make it clear that you recognize responsibility for what went wrong, and that you are sincere in remorse and in taking steps to rectify a situation. Bad apologies appear insincere, try to shift blame, or avoid true responsibility.

United Airlines was much criticized for its initial statements in the wake of a paying passenger being dragged off an airplane as the airline decided to give his seat to another, presumably higher-value passenger.[13] United's CEO initially put out an internal memo that seemed to blame the customer and the following public statement that was perceived as tone deaf under the circumstances:

> This is an upsetting event to all of us here at United. I apologize for having to re-accommodate these customers. Our team is moving with a sense of urgency to work with the authorities and conduct our own detailed review of what happened. We are also reaching out to this passenger to talk directly to him and further address and resolve this situation. —Oscar Munoz, CEO, United Airlines

After considerable criticism and attendant reflection, the CEO issued the following, more personal, and more effective message:

> The truly horrific event that occurred on this flight has elicited many responses from all of us: outrage, anger, disappointment. I share all of those sentiments, and one above all: my deepest apologies for what happened. Like you, I continue to be disturbed by what happened on this flight and I deeply apologize to the customer forcibly removed and to all the customers aboard. No one should ever be mistreated this way. I want you to know that we take full responsibility, and we will work to make it right. It's never too late to do the right thing. I have committed to our customers and our employees that we are going to fix what's broken, so this never happens again. This will include a thorough review of crew movement, our policies for incentivizing volunteers in these situations, how we handle oversold situations and an examination of how we partner with airport authorities and local law enforcement. We'll communicate the results of our review by April 30th. I promise you we will do better.

At its most basic level, if your apology would not impress your spouse or grandmother, it is not going to do any better with your corporate constituencies. The point is to get permission to change the conversation and begin a new one.

Because good apologies make it clear that you are owning up to responsibility for a situation, they can sometimes create tension with lawyers who are trying to minimize potential liability. Increasingly, however, even lawyers recognize that there can be significant brand and reputation value destruction when an apology "looks like it was written by the lawyers." More and more, executives and their lawyers understand that the trade-off just isn't worth it.

Do you apologize before you have all the facts? Sometimes it is patently clear that a company did something wrong and violated legal or social norms. When this is obvious in the inner concentric circles, you can be sure it is obvious to the outer rings. That is when to consider a "holding apology." This acknowledges that we know there is an issue, we are sorry for any impact, and we are investigating how it came about and what we expect to do about it. If there are clear mitigation steps that can be taken, communicate them. If not, promise to keep communicating as more is known and appropriate.

See Chapter 9 for more on apologies.

Developing Third-Party Friends Before a Crisis

One of the most common asks in a crisis is whether it is possible to identify friendly third parties to weigh in with positive commentary around the handling of the situation. Examples include friendly analysts and investors, academics, industry experts, management gurus, and politicians. This always sounds good, but it is one of the most difficult challenges during an actual crisis. Credible third parties who have enough information to opine credibly, and who are willing to stick their necks out for no pay, are few and far between. Pay them and they have less credibility and are therefore less useful. Much like social media, having friendly third parties in your corner takes significant effort to cultivate in peacetime. This is worth doing. Starting from scratch in a crisis is rarely a useful game changer.

Understanding What People Want and Need to Hear and from Whom

All audiences in a crisis want to hear that the crisis is being managed as a priority. They want to know that competent people are focused on its resolution and that you are working to mitigate and redress impact as much as humanly possible. It is important to inform your internal audiences and—as much as possible—keep communicating to them so they are capable of articulating to outside parties (including family and friends) that they believe you are taking the right steps. Your workforce should be your most effective outside ambassadors for your organization. This places a premium on communications to them. Live town halls, conference calls, group meetings, and so on are powerful and should be part of your arsenal along with videos, emails, and social media. In a long-running situation, surveys and focus groups can be extremely helpful in taking the temperature of your organization.

Similarly, surveys of your outside audiences are a critical tool to ensure that your messaging is addressing their questions and concerns and that it is positively shaping perceptions of how you are managing a crisis.

Can We Keep This Out of the Press?

Not every "crisis" is necessarily newsworthy but, in a content-hungry, click-driven media world, bad news tastes especially good. In many cases, especially for publicly traded or highly regulated companies, you won't have a choice around whether or not to disclose and communicate broadly about an issue, via press release, 8-K, or conference call, on an accelerated basis.

Judgments around continuing press interest and your efforts to avoid a "drip, drip, drip" of news—which keeps a story alive—are some of the most difficult and nuanced. Being proactive—either directly through your own social channels or "getting ahead of a story" by engaging with a reporter or two who may be willing to inject balance—is a delicate judgment call. Ultimately it will come down to whether you think you have enough information to be reasonably complete, and whether the story will hold until you do. Is the issue universally known internally? Are there potential whistleblowers who might force your hand? Does an investor, customer, competitor, or former employee have motivation to feed the story to a favored reporter?

What About Advertising?

Probably the fastest way to get a controlled message out to the broader public is by placing an open letter in major newspapers and linking it to social media. These messages vary from acknowledging a problem and committing to do something about it, to post-crisis efforts to say the issue has been addressed and committing to re-earn trust. Of course, not every crisis has a national or international constituency, and so you wouldn't do this if you can be more targeted.

But when a broad audience needs to get facts, have key questions answered, or be instructed to do something, the "open letter" can make a useful impression. Most effective when short and to the point, this tool is quick to execute, effective, and direct. Your messaging is unfiltered by editorial opinion. The risk of course is that it can raise a profile and draw people into the discussion that might not have been focused on your issue. Your messaging will receive extra, highly skeptical scrutiny and needs to be developed with that in mind. Focus group testing before you place advertising is critical.

One other word on advertising. Be careful about being accused of "trying to advertise your way out of a crisis." This is especially true of more brand-oriented advertising. Starting brand-oriented or "feel good" advertising too early can be as dangerous as failing to pull an obviously tone-deaf campaign in the middle of a crisis.

Legislators and Regulators

Every company and institution must have in today's world a communications plan to engage with its regulators and legislators. In a crisis, they expect to hear from you early and often. They do not like surprises or reading about things in the press.

In a crisis, you need to have senior executives on the phone and in person with updates on a regular cadence. In a high-profile situation, the potential for being required to give testimony increases. Always plan messaging from the beginning of any crisis with a view to how it will play with this audience, and to what questions they will ask in a committee or Congressional hearing.

Summary

When faced with a crisis, put yourself in the shoes of those who are affected. Move quickly. Minutes and hours count. Decide first what needs to be done rather than what needs to be said. When you have a plan, tell your constituents honestly and as completely as you can what they need to know and what you are doing to resolve the situation or to make amends. Move decisively. Be human. Avoid platitudes and legalese. Be engaged and BE SEEN as engaged. Before a crisis happens, assess how you communicate to all your constituents and think about how you would prioritize and leverage those channels if needed. In other words, prepare! Treat the press courteously but with caution. The press should not be the primary channel through which you communicate. But, if you have developed strong relationships with certain reporters, prioritize them to keep them close and benefit from their insights and critiques.

8

What About Our People? Human Resources Aspects

All corporations operate with a variety of types of capital: financial, physical (property, plant, and equipment), intellectual (patents, trademarks, and trade secrets), reputational, and human. Along with financial and reputational capital, human capital may be the most vulnerable to damage or loss in a crisis. And that vulnerability may be highly dependent upon which of the four categories of crisis (described in Chapter 1) is being addressed.

As discussed in Chapter 4, leaders of a crisis management team need to pay particular, but certainly not exclusive, attention to those colleagues who may be thought of as being at Ground Zero of a crisis—those who may have been, or feel, responsible for a crisis in Category #1 or #2; whistleblowers; and those who are tasked with key roles in directly addressing a crisis in any category or who take on additional responsibilities to keep normal operations on track.

One of the first questions that gets asked about anyone who may have been responsible for actions that precipitated a Category #1 or #2 crisis is this: should he or she be fired? The likely answer is "no," at least until there can be a clear understanding that they were actually the cause (not just "may have been"). Another factor relevant to a firing decision is whether the actions taken by the individual were intentional, reckless, grossly negligent, or a simple mistake that could happen to just about anyone. It can take some time to reach a conclusion about that. Nevertheless, such a person is likely to be personally in crisis, especially if the person has been informed that he or she is a target or subject of a grand jury or has received a "Wells Notice" from the SEC. (A Wells Notice is a letter from the regulator giving an individual a warning that the regulator is considering bringing charges and inviting the individual to submit an explanation for why charges would not be warranted.) Anyone who has received any such notification may not be able to fully function in his or her regular role, so the best thing for that person and the company may be a leave of absence, likely with pay for at least some period of time.

A leave of absence will also allow such a person to spend the time necessary to address a crisis-related investigation—either an internal investigation or one conducted by regulatory or criminal authorities. Unfortunately, a short-sighted response to being the focus of an investigation or even just being interviewed is to be less than truthful or candid and, even, to attempt to destroy documents. For this reason, a company should take early steps to preserve documents in the possession or control of anyone who may be a focus of an investigation. IT and forensic consultants may need to be retained if there is a concern that documents may be, or have been, destroyed. Also, legal counsel should be provided to that person in order to encourage him or her to be forthcoming. If a person on leave (or any other employee) is not cooperative, that will likely lead to a termination of employment, and often company policies provide for such an outcome. A dicier version of this question arises when an employee is brought before a grand jury or other criminal authority and invokes the Fifth Amendment. As a general proposition, a private employer is allowed to terminate an employee who "takes the Fifth."

The facts underlying a crisis in Category #1 or #2 are often brought to the attention of management or a board by a whistleblower. Because of the myriad laws and regulations prohibiting retaliatory actions against whistleblowers, it is critical that management be admonished not to take any actions that could credibly be alleged to constitute retaliation. Indeed, when a whistleblower is anonymous (as is often the case), it would be a mistake even to try to ascertain his or her identity.[1]

Then there is the group on the front lines of managing the crisis. The combination of time demands and associated stress is a recipe for burnout if the crisis, as is often the case, has a long duration. Left unaddressed, that can impede optimal performance in managing the crisis, and also create a risk of loss of their services in the post-crisis period. As indicated above, there will also be a group that is playing a vital role in managing normal operations. Individuals in this category are often subject to increased time demands and, on occasion, feel the stress of additional responsibilities for which they may not feel qualified—again, creating a risk of burnout.

Another category of colleagues to whom special attention should be paid are customer- and public-facing employees. Depending upon the circumstances, they may be on the receiving end of critical comments or even harassment, which will clearly have an impact on morale and possibly job performance. That could also lead those colleagues to intemperate reactions toward outsiders that could be bad for business.

Low morale can be an issue for just about any employee of a company in crisis. When the crisis is in Category #1 or #2, their pride in working for the company may be replaced by embarrassment—especially if the company is prominent enough to attract a good deal of media attention. Even well-meaning comments of friends and family meant to express supportiveness can have the opposite effect. One of the best antidotes for this issue is excellent pre-crisis reputation management and effective mid-crisis external communications. In an extreme case, a Category #3 or #4 crisis can lead to something akin to PTSD. In the case of companies in the World Trade Center that were dealing with the fallout of 9/11, some of their employees who worked in the Towers suffered from actual PTSD, whether or not they were in the building at the time of the attacks. Well-run companies directly affected by 9/11 provided on-site counseling for their employees. They also considered the concerns of family members (especially children) who were anxious about having a parent or spouse return to work in Manhattan when there was the possibility of a follow-on attack. There were laudable CEOs who attended funerals and who communicated with sincerity and empathy to employees and to the families of those who lost their lives or were seriously injured.

Again, in extreme cases, morale can also be negatively impacted by the anxiety of not knowing whether the employer will be able to survive. Even those who feel that their company will survive may worry about layoffs that a company may need to do in order to preserve liquidity or address reduced demand for its products or services. Those who are not laid off will miss their colleagues and may worry about being in the "next round." Comforting internal communications will be useful in addressing this issue, but only if the facts will support whatever is said and the internal and external communications (including SEC disclosures) are in alignment. Truthfulness—even, or especially, involving tough messages—is critical.

Of course, sometimes layoffs cannot be avoided, but they must be done with care so as to avoid, or best be prepared for, legal claims and adverse publicity. Companies will need to comply with the provisions of the Worker Adjustment and Retraining Notification (WARN) Act and similar state laws. In summary, that Act requires most employers of 100 or more employees to provide 60 days' notice of a "mass layoff," as defined. They should take care to avoid disproportionately affecting employees in protected categories—for example, minorities and those covered by the Age Act. One way to do this is through a statistical analysis that assesses whether those individuals are being laid off at a greater rate than would be expected given the relevant employee population. And then there is the risk of adverse publicity. For example, if a company is engaging in a layoff and at the same time has a stock buyback program that hasn't been halted or its senior executives have attracted attention for high compensation levels or lavish perks, both the company and its leadership should expect to be attacked in the press and on social media. Or, if the company compares unfavorably with peers in terms of its severance policy, that fact will not escape attention. All of this can lead to morale issues among employees who are not being laid off.

Morale issues open the door for poaching of employees by competitors. This can be exacerbated when stock options and other equity-based compensation are an important part of the overall compensation package and lose their value as a result of crisis-related stock price drops. Of course, even an option that is "underwater" can have value under a Black-Scholes analysis. (A Black-Scholes analysis is a Nobel Prize–winning mathematical calculation of the value of an option. In the case of an employee stock option, the analysis recognizes that, on the date of grant of the option, there is value being delivered to the employee despite the fact that the exercise price on that date is equal to the then-market price of the underlying security. If the market price drops below the exercise price [and is "underwater"], there can still be value because the market price can go above the exercise price before the option expires.) But from a retention standpoint, that notion requires some degree of faith on the part of the option holder that the price will recover before the expiration date. Concerns of this sort may lead to a management recommendation to a board to re-price options. Option re-pricing can be effected by a variety of means—exchanges, cash buyouts, and amendments. But it has some degree of complexity as a governance, regulatory, tax, and accounting matter, and can also have significant investor relations implications. Another alternative for employee retention in the midst of a crisis is to establish a cash retention pool. However, when the crisis is in Category #1 or #2, this should be done cautiously, because shareholders, regulators, and others might object to the appearance of increasing pay for individuals who might be thought to have caused or contributed to the crisis. Recall the uproar when AIG paid out over $200 million in bonuses to individuals in its financial services division who allegedly caused that company's issues in the period before 2008 by negligently insuring toxic assets. This despite the facts that AIG was contractually obligated to do so and that the individuals were needed to help solve the crisis.[2]

In some instances, cash compensation might actually be reduced during a crisis. This may be effected across the board to preserve liquidity. Or, when operational imperatives require furloughs and layoffs, the executive team might take reductions as a symbol of solidarity. The latter step might be viewed with some cynicism if at about the same time the executive team receives large option grants at strike prices that are thought to be temporarily depressed due to the crisis.[3]

In some ways, the ultimate HR issue for a company in crisis arises when the board has lost faith in the CEO, either because of the actions that led to the crisis or because of his or her management of the crisis. Even when the board continues to support a CEO, a change in that position may effectively be forced upon it by shareholders. And a change in the CEO may be required to obtain support for the company's plan of reorganization (if, as described in Chapter 5, it was compelled to file bankruptcy) or to avoid the imposition of a monitor (as described in Chapter 6). When the board has reached the conclusion that the CEO must go, it is confronted with a series of questions:

- Should this be "effective immediately"?
- When it is not effective immediately, when must the conclusion be disclosed?
- Who will step in, on either a permanent or an interim basis?
- What will be the impact of the removal of the CEO, and the naming of a member of the team as a replacement, on the remainder of the management team?
- What are the terms of the CEO's contract relating to termination?
- What will be the difference from a financial standpoint between a "for cause" and a "not for cause" termination, and does the board have an appropriate factual and legal basis for deciding between the two?
- If the board believes it has "cause," but the CEO disputes that characterization, can the payment of any amounts of severance be deferred pending the resolution of that disagreement through litigation or (if the employment agreement so provides) arbitration? If there is to be a deferral of payment, must the amounts in dispute be set aside in a trust or escrow?
- How might the financial payout be affected if we allow the CEO to resign rather than being fired?
- Under what circumstances should we allow the CEO to resign rather than being fired?
- What will be the reaction of shareholders, employees, and the financial press to whatever payout is made, whether or not mandated by the contract?
- Is the termination of the CEO a deemed resignation by him or her from the board?
- Is the CEO required for some period not to compete with the company?

- Is the CEO required to cooperate with any investigation and not disparage the company or any of its employees, officers, and directors?
- Is the company going to be required to indemnify the CEO, and also to advance expenses, and so on?
- What do we say in our press release about the CEO and the reason for the termination? And, are we going to have to deal with recent, pre-termination expressions of "full support" of the CEO by the board?
- What will be the impact of the removal of the CEO on pending litigation and/or regulatory proceedings?

If the termination is mandated by personal misbehavior by the CEO (e.g., a #MeToo issue and any other serious violation of a code of conduct), it can be a huge mistake for a board to express anything resembling sympathy toward the CEO or regret at having to take the action. To do so could be counter-cultural, damage relationships with the employees, and possibly be used in a proxy contest or withhold campaign by shareholders. It would amount to an "anti-apology" by the company. It can also be a mistake under those circumstances to fail to be candid and call the termination a "retirement" or use some other euphemism. The real reason will inevitably come out.

When a CEO (or any other high-level employee) is terminated, a company and the terminated individual will often enter into an agreement covering a number of subjects beyond financial arrangements—subjects such as confidentiality and non-disparagement. Ever since the 2015 ruling against Kellogg Brown & Root in a case brought by the SEC, companies have been careful to include exceptions to the requirements of such provisions in employment or termination agreements to make it clear that they could not be interpreted as measures to prohibit or discourage employees from reporting securities law violations to the SEC.[4]

In addition, when a CEO has been terminated, his or her successor should be cautioned about the downside of publicly (or privately but quotably) criticizing the terminated CEO. This may be a contractual requirement if the non-disparagement provision in a CEO's severance agreement is mutual. But it is also a matter of common sense—the outgoing CEO may still have supporters running important functions; a criticism might suggest faulty previous public disclosure or failure of board oversight.

As reflected in the notion of concentric circles of communications described in Chapter 7, it is critical to focus on the company's own people when managing a crisis.

9

What About That Apology?
A Multifaceted Issue

While the subject of apologies was addressed succinctly in the chapter on communications, it is worth pausing over again at the end of this Part II. The subject can be used to illustrate the intersection (and occasional collision) of the various aspects of executing crisis management. The subject also has an impact on reputation rehabilitation, to be discussed in Part III, and can be an important step toward reasserting the company's commitment to values that it claims to be aspects of its culture.

There are four issues to consider in a discussion of apologies: Do we make one? What do we say? When do we say it? Who delivers it? There can be a robust debate among the various disciplines about how to answer each of these questions, and it will be up to the leader of the crisis management team (presumably the CEO) to mediate among the views being expressed. And the answers might differ depending upon the category of crisis being dealt with.

To Apologize or Not. In dealing with most of the crises in Category #1, there is likely to be little debate about the appropriateness of issuing an apology. The principal advocates for issuing an apology will likely be the business leaders and communications professionals who are most concerned about the company's reputation. As described in Chapter 7, lawyers who are focused on defending the company against liability might be expected to argue against an apology out of a concern that it could be viewed as an admission of responsibility. Lawyers who are advising on SEC disclosures will also ponder the implications of an apology. But even the lawyers will support making an apology, although they will be quite focused on the words to be used. Others interested in the words to be used are those members of the team responsible for financial reporting (who will be thinking about reserve setting), those who interact with lending sources and auditors, and those who oversee the insurance program (who will ponder the underwriters' reactions).

There can be more of a debate over apologizing for a Category #2 crisis. After all, the facts that result in that kind of crisis did not result from normal operations or the pursuit of the company's strategy. That type of crisis is more subject to a "violation of company policy" explanation. And in a Category #3 crisis there will be those who will argue, "why should a victim apologize?" In these kinds of crises, the lawyers might argue that an apology connotes a greater degree of responsibility on the part of the company than is appropriate under the circumstances. Nevertheless, because important constituencies are adversely affected by the facts underlying these types of crises, some expression of regret would seem to be in order. And a failure to say something along these lines would likely make the company a noticeable outlier, given the number of other companies that have had to deal with similar issues.

What Do We Say? Clearly in the case of a Category #1 crisis, the "impress your grandmother" and "don't make it look like it was written by lawyers" tests described in Chapter 7 provide the correct standard. This view is supported by the advice from CEOs that we report on at the end of Chapter 12. There may be something of a temptation to attribute the cause of even a Category #1 crisis to a "rogue employee." While that might be accurate and even the right thing to do, it should be carefully considered. Such an approach may run counter to the grandma/not-lawyers tests. It may also have other downsides. As a legal matter, it doesn't really help with civil liability, because the acts of an employee are the acts of the company. Period. (It may, however, mitigate or reduce the risk of punitive damages in a civil suit and reduce the risk of criminal liability.) And, an identified rogue employee might dispute the assertion that he or she was involved (and even file a defamation claim) or dispute the assertion of "rogueness" (by claiming that supervisors knew or encouraged the behavior). As an HR matter, it might create a morale issue; the employee's colleagues might use terms like "scapegoat" or "under the bus."

In the case of a Category #2 crisis, it would seem appropriate and fair to speak of a violation of policy, if true. In the case of a #MeToo situation, it would also be appropriate to lament the fact that any employee was subjected to bad behavior. But, again, be wary of potential pushback. The lamentation could trigger "you knew this was going on" responses, exacerbated if the terminated employee is given a rich severance package. In the case of a Category #3 crisis, a statement recognizing that certain constituencies have been inconvenienced (say, by a cyberattack) may be a sufficient apology, especially if the company believes that its efforts to avoid the event were generally state of the art.

When Do We Apologize? In most instances, the answer is as soon as possible. As indicated in Chapter 7, there may be a benefit in saying something even before all of the facts are known—the "holding apology." But that should be followed up with more communication after the facts have been fleshed out.

Who Delivers the Apology? Clearly, the CEO is the default messenger. To select anyone else subjects both the company and the CEO to criticism. That said, the apology must be well scripted and delivered with discipline—no ad-libbing. Remember that the "get my life back" comment that contributed to the CEO of BP losing his job was made during the delivery of an apology about the Gulf oil spill disaster.

* * *

An apology implicates virtually all of the aspects of executing crisis management that are discussed in Part II—the CEO will need to mediate differing views of his or her multidisciplinary team, an apology is a key part of the communications strategy, and it has potential legal, financial, and HR implications. In preparing the language of the apology, it should be remembered that it will be heard by both internal and external constituencies. There is one last point to consider, as part of the "who calls the shots" question. While the CEO and the internal and outside members of the team will need to consider the four questions discussed above, it is clearly appropriate for the CEO to consult with the board of directors before issuing (or concluding not to issue) an apology. There is too much at stake for the CEO, personally, and the company to do otherwise.

Finally, an apology may be a critical first step in reputation rehabilitation, a subject of Part III.

· III ·

Recover

10

Why Did It Happen?
Root Cause Analysis

Thoughtful companies that have experienced an adverse event will engage in a retrospective analysis to understand why it happened, largely to prevent a recurrence. For example, if a company has experienced a sudden loss of sales, it needs to understand whether it has a quality problem of its own making or whether a competitor has developed a superior product or manner of doing business. If a company has lost a number of valuable employees, it needs to understand if it is driving away people due to a toxic culture or whether it has fallen far behind on compensation and/or benefits. That kind of analysis is appropriate in respect of adverse events that do not rise to the level of a crisis, but it is even more important when there has been a crisis—at least a crisis that falls into Category #1 or #2. In many ways, it is the first step in modifying and fortifying post-crisis risk management—the critical element of preparedness for the next crisis.

The best kind of retrospective analysis is a root cause analysis (RCA), because it looks deeply into the fundamental cause of the crisis. There seem to be about as many books and articles written about RCAs as there are books about crisis communications.[1] The typical process to follow in an RCA involves the following steps:[2]

- Assemble a multidisciplinary team—this might be the same team that was assembled to manage the crisis.
- Define the problem—in the case of an RCA of a crisis, this may be self-evident.
- Identify the contributing factors—that is, what were the more-or-less direct causes of the crisis; the three basic types are physical, human, and organizational. Human and organizational factors can clearly include a defective culture.
- Identify the "root cause" that allowed or caused the contributing factors to develop into a crisis; this identification often involves asking "why?" five times (an example follows).

- Determine what changes are required to eliminate the identified root cause.
- Figure out how to monitor the implementation and measure the success of those changes.

The results of the RCA (and especially the last two elements) should be shared with the board of directors.

To illustrate the RCA approach, take the hypothetical situation of a food producer that had to work through a crisis (financial, legal, and reputational) caused by contaminated products. The problem can be stated simply as "our products have made people very sick." (A caveat: this is a purely hypothetical illustration. There can certainly be other, and less damning, causes of food contamination and more benign answers to the five whys.) The "five whys" might be as follows: Why #1—Because we allowed bacteria to fester in our plants. Why #2—Because the plant personnel did not place enough emphasis on cleaning our equipment. Why #3—Because the general manager of the plant did not want to add cleaning and inspecting personnel or, during periods of high demand, take the plant offline periodically for deep cleaning. Why #4—Because in a period of high demand, senior corporate management were pushing the plant manager for output, did not emphasize the higher priority of a safety culture, and failed to take seriously a whistleblower complaint. Why #5—Because the board did not provide sufficient oversight on this area of compliance.

The changes that might be made in light of this litany might start with corporate governance matters. These would include a change in board oversight processes and compensation design to emphasize safety and a requirement that any whistleblower complaint be reported to the board. In the case of a "mission critical" issue (such as food safety), such a complaint should be reported immediately. The answers to the "five whys" may also unearth shortcomings in a variety of areas: in corporate culture, in management structure (such as silos or excessive decentralization),[3] in compensation design, or in quality control. The answers may lead to changes in each.

The medical profession and hospitals have long engaged in RCAs— they call them M&M (for "morbidity and mortality") conferences. These are held to understand the reasons for adverse events in patient care and to identify steps to prevent recurrences. They are described as "non-punitive" and are generally privileged and confidential as a matter of law. A corporate RCA does not necessarily have these attributes. It is possible that the answers given above in the "five whys" hypothetical would lead to termination of, or other employment action against, individuals who were involved. And, depending upon how that hypothetical RCA were to be conducted, the final conclusion and subsidiary answers may not be privileged. Nevertheless, an RCA relating to a crisis should be a business imperative.

For some types of crisis, an RCA might even be a legal imperative. For example, in December 2017, the Department of Justice adopted a new policy relating to enforcement of the Foreign Corrupt Practices Act (FCPA). The policy gives companies "credit" (that is, an opportunity to reduce the consequences of a violation) for a number of actions, including "timely and appropriate remediation." However, "to receive full credit" for remediation, a company must, among other things, provide a "Demonstration of thorough analysis of causes of underlying conduct (i.e., a root cause analysis) and, where appropriate, remediation to address the root cause."[4] A "second cousin" of an RCA is an assessment of the corporation's compliance program. As noted in Chapter 2, a really bad set of facts can lead to criminal exposure, and an effort to adopt a new compliance program, or improve an existing one, can have an impact on whether the company is to be charged criminally.

Similarly, root cause analyses are encouraged or required by various regulatory bodies: the Occupational Safety and Health Administration of the Department of Labor (OSHA) and the Environmental Protection Agency (EPA), in the case of "incident investigations"; the Federal Aviation Agency (FAA), National Aeronautics and Space Administration (NASA), and National Transportation Safety Board (NTSB), in the case of transportation accidents; the US Department of Agriculture (USDA) and Centers for Disease Control and Prevention (CDC), in the event of foodborne illnesses; and so on. So, one of the questions for boards and managements to ask counsel is whether there is, indeed, a legal mandate for an RCA following a crisis.

Whether an RCA is undertaken as a business imperative or because of a legal mandate, two questions are worth pausing over—when and how should the RCA be conducted?

In the event of a crisis that has the potential for a recurrence in the near term, it seems logical as a business matter to begin the RCA as soon as possible. Of course, immediacy may be compelled when an RCA is legally mandated.

Otherwise, there could be an argument for deferral of the RCA for at least a short period. The management of a crisis is hugely time consuming and stressful. Because many of the people to be involved in the RCA will have been deeply involved in the management of the crisis, it may be useful to allow them to catch their breath—both physically and to allow for thoughtful reflection and take some of the emotion out of the RCA process. In addition, as discussed in Chapter 6, there can be many forms of pending legal proceedings ongoing. An RCA has the potential for creating a record that will make the defense of those proceedings more difficult. And the findings of the adversaries in the discovery portion of such proceedings might actually be pertinent input to the RCA itself and should be reported to the board.

Regardless of the decision about the timing of the RCA, it is not simply a brainstorming exercise. The RCA process will have many of the attributes of an internal investigation. Steps should be taken to preserve relevant documents (although that will already need to be done if there are threatened or pending legal proceedings). Employees and others who will be interviewed should be encouraged to provide full cooperation and candid answers. A decision will need to be made about who (management and/or members of the board) will direct the analysis and whether to involve outsiders (lawyers and/or consultants). When conclusions have been reached, careful thought should be given to the form of the report on those conclusions. And when remedial steps are proposed in those conclusions, decisions will need to be made about the implementation of those steps and how and when to audit that implementation. Consideration should be given to management incentives and rewards for successful implementation and, conversely, negative consequences for a failure to succeed in that implementation in a timely fashion.

Last point about an RCA: focused too narrowly, an RCA can be like military preparing to fight the last war. Of course, it should assist in preventing a recurrence of the crisis that just happened, but that is a baseline purpose. The lessons from an RCA about a past crisis of a specific type should also be generalized and extrapolated from to be useful in averting other types of crises. For example, around the time of its 2010 settlement of the ABACUS CDO matter (for $550 million), Goldman Sachs created a Business Standards Committee operating under the oversight of its board of directors. Its mandate was to look at "six important areas for detailed examination based on the events and developments in recent years." Presumably, ABACUS was one of those "events and developments." The Committee issued its report in 2011 and issued an "impact report" two years later declaring that recommendations in the report had been implemented. One of the key underlying themes identified in the impact report was "reputational sensitivity and awareness."[5] The Goldman RCA was broader than ABACUS and also served as reputational rehabilitation of the type discussed in Chapter 11.

11

Can We Regain Trust?
Reputation Rehabilitation

Well before a crisis has passed is the time to begin thinking about and planning for reputation rehabilitation. How you handle your crisis—more than the fact of the crisis itself—is often more determinative of how your constituents regard you afterward, and how to engage in an effective rehab effort.

As discussed in Chapter 7, if you think of your constituents in terms of concentric circles of influence, your rehabilitation effort will similarly begin with an effort to ensure that each group has had its questions answered and believes that management has competently addressed and managed the issues underlying the crisis. If anyone in your concentric circles has unanswered questions, that can undermine a long-term recovery plan.

At its core, reputation rehab is the effort to convince your constituents that what happened was an anomaly—that you learned from what happened, took it seriously, took responsibility for addressing it, and have taken appropriate steps—to a reasonable extent—to ensure it doesn't happen again. It might also include commitments that go beyond the actual crisis that put you on a better path to be a better organization over the long term.

Remarkably, there's been very little written about reputation rehabilitation. Most literature focuses—as does this book—on planning, reacting, and managing in the heat of battle. A notable exception is a short blog post from the International Association of Business Communicators (IABC) in which an unnamed author notes that they were also unable to find much about the topic.[1]

The five stages the IABC outlines are what it calls the five "Rs": "recognize," "recalibrate," "repair," "redirect," and "reinvigorate."

On the first, "Recognize," the IABC says that determining the official "end" to a crisis depends on its severity. Essentially, one must recognize when a crisis peak has passed and the adrenaline rush of crisis response is declining.

Put in more colloquial terms, when has the "hair on fire" phase passed?

Are you in the "grind it out" phase, the period where the core actions have been mostly decided and which requires longer-term strategic thinking and a programmatic—rather than immediately reactive—posture? Have you transitioned into a dangerous finger-pointing and accountability phase, where corporate infighting and political jockeying over what happened can sometimes undermine or derail a sense of progress? And do you have sufficient visibility into what you would like the end stage to look like? Importantly, have you achieved the necessary stability to begin a concerted recovery?

The "recalibrate" stage encourages organizations to "assess the damage" by understanding and measuring the impact of the crisis on the organization's business. While the IABC focuses mainly on media metrics, it's clear that, to get a comprehensive picture, formal and informal research across all constituencies is essential and worth the investment, before, during, and after a crisis.

Understanding what your constituencies think and setting benchmarks is a vital part of any communications effort. If you don't know what they really think—and exactly how your reputation has been damaged—you can't gauge and measure the effectiveness of your rehabilitation efforts. Put another way, if you don't know where you are, it's hard to tell where you are going and how.

The next step suggested in the IABC blog is "repair," with the recommendation that organizations "articulate a strategy" that will "lead the company on a path toward normalization." In 2018 in Philadelphia, Starbucks was under fire after two African American men were arrested for not ordering anything while waiting for a friend. IABC points out two measures that Starbucks took in its repair phase: firing the store manager, and then arranging meetings with the CEO, the two men who were detained, and relevant advocacy groups.[2] The long-term strategy "included an overhaul of corporate policies and mandatory anti-bias training at 8,000 U.S. stores the month following the incident." In Boeing's case (see Chapter 7), among other things, they established a new board-level committee, reorganized the engineering function, did a culture review, and held several leaders accountable.

The fourth stage, "redirect," argues that organizations should take proactive steps to communicate change and progress, rather than just provide "reactive responses" to inbound questions.

Finally, the last stage, "reinvigorate," urges that corporations take measures to reinforce "brand values and relationships" that may have deteriorated as a result of the crisis. So many times, in a crisis, the cracks that had been forming in an organization's culture and adherence to professed values become glaringly obvious. It's critical to ask questions about whether or not the culture encourages or discourages people coming forward with problems. Ask yourself how your organization solicits observations and input from employees and external constituents about where actual behaviors deviate from professed values. If you don't have a good feel for any disconnects, solving them will be impossible.

Each Crisis Is Different

As mentioned several times in this book, all crises are different. The challenges around reputation rehabilitation are also different depending on whether the crisis was something internally generated and core to your business (the first of the four categories described in Chapter 1), or internally generated but not directly impacting operations or the core mission of the company (e.g., an isolated communications lapse or #MeToo with a senior executive), or it is something external that happens to you (Categories #3 and #4).

When a crisis is "done to you"—that is, you have been impacted by some external event over which you have little initial control—the focus is always going to be mostly on the quality of your response.

For example, Procter & Gamble learned one day that teenagers were eating and filming themselves eating Tide Pods laundry detergent.[3] The "Tide Pod Challenge" went viral and thousands of young people, including toddlers, were poisoning themselves. Capital One Bank discovered that a former employee insider had compromised its security by stealing customer data.[4] McDonald's, IHOP, and many other restaurant chains have been forced to deal with random acts of violence.

In these cases, the companies acted swiftly to show that they took the problem seriously, that they were reasonably prepared to manage the issue, and that they were acting responsibly to address it. A well-managed incident response can reinforce the quality of management or highlight disorganization and weak leadership. Even when there are slight fumbles, being able to communicate that you have learned from events and that you are now better placed to manage them in the future will usually increase confidence.

If the crisis is something you could have seen coming and failed to prepare for (e.g., a cyberattack), your rehabilitation effort will be more challenging. While bad things happen to good companies through no fault of their own—and that can engender some sympathy—the quality, speed, and comprehensiveness of the response will be judged independently and will either enhance or detract from your reputation.

More difficult for any organization is when a crisis is driven by internal—sometimes cultural—failings that had been unrecognized or ignored until too late, for example, driving profits at the expense of safety (BP), competitive pressures, overstretched manufacturing lines, fraying supplier relations and an arrogant engineering culture (Boeing), or simply undetected bad or criminal behavior.

Especially in circumstances where your organization's own failings, or misbehavior or lapses of judgment by a senior executive, are part of the root cause (for example, McDonald's ex-CEO Steve Easterbrook), rehabilitation must start from the top.[5] Board engagement is critical, and independent reviews into how a situation occurred are becoming standard operating procedure. They are a critical step in dimensionalizing the issue and pointing the way to necessary changes that will convince your audiences that the root causes of a problem have been identified and addressed.

In large-scale disaster situations, for example, Pacific Gas & Electric fires and pipeline explosions in California, or the Boeing 737 MAX crashes, you can never really put the event completely behind you. The expectation is that—somehow—the organization will memorialize the event in some way so that the lessons learned are never forgotten. Boeing, for instance, has institutionalized living memorials to those lost in the 737 MAX crashes.

If the crisis is internally generated around something core to your business and raises questions about culture, quality, competence, or judgment, reputational rehab will be a longer road. It will require significant introspection as to how the crisis happened and what changes need to be made to ensure it doesn't happen again. Indeed, a silver lining from this, for many companies, can be that it can make you a better company going forward, even though the process itself may be painful. If the crisis relates to bad behavior by an executive, demonstrating that such behavior is an anomaly and inconsistent with company values and norms will be crucial.

When a crisis is generated by some internal failing or mistake, constituent focus is going to be on root cause and your ability to learn and change as a result. You will need to be thoughtful and strategic around how and when to communicate your commitment to make the changes and to demonstrate progress in achieving them.

Evaluating and Understanding Impact on Reputation

Crises can consume extraordinary amounts of executive and board time and attention. Sometimes they are relatively minor issues that can be dealt with expeditiously with little fallout. Sometimes they are existential and threaten the survival of the company or organization. Recognizing and deciding where a crisis is on that spectrum is the starting point for any post "hair on fire" effort. Obviously, the work done in the initial reaction phase can help you get a leg up on recovery. Or, if the initial response was bungled, it can mean you have a deeper hole from which to climb out.

Ask yourself, who knows about the problem? What do they think caused the problem? Did you react appropriately, taking into account the constituencies who are most vested in seeing the problem resolved? Are all of your constituencies impacted in similar or different ways? Do they believe you have taken the appropriate steps to avoid a recurrence?

Your concentric circles (as discussed in Chapter 7) may be a useful guide as you assess reputation impact—or you may need to reorder them, depending on the impact a crisis has had on each circle. Conduct research directly with the groups most affected. Have they lowered their opinion of your company? Is the crisis one that they blame you and your company for? Is it something they think you could have avoided with forethought? Do they have issues with tone at the top? Do they think you are focused on the right things?

Consider a mix of traditional surveys and focus groups to get at how people really view your company or organization, how they rate leadership, and what they would like to see from the company going forward. Research is the best way to make sure you are focusing your resources on the actual problem you have, which is very often quite different from the problem you think you have. Properly conceived, research also gives you a benchmark against which you can measure progress and set goals, which can make you a better company over the long term. Put more simply, make sure you are learning from what happened and applying the lessons.

"Let's Put This Behind Us."

Once upon a time, these were cherished words in crisis communications. Let's face it, everyone wants to move on from a problem. But while the sentiment is worthy, the best reputation rehab efforts include some kind of articulation of how an event has changed you and your organization— ideally for the better! Most commonly today, people want to see how a crisis and its resolution are baked into institutional learning and memory, and how tangible changes have resulted—or will result. Words such as "Let's put this behind us" or—as the CEO of BP said in an unguarded moment—"I want my life back" are tone deaf and can undermine the sense of seriousness with which you are taking the situation.

Failing to learn from crisis increases the chances of another crisis, and it makes efforts to recover from a subsequent crisis much harder.

Independent Investigations and Assessments

Independent investigations are not for every situation, but they are a useful key tactic in beginning a rehabilitation process. Engaging and announcing a credible, independent third party to review and report on what happened can quickly underscore an organization's commitment to transparency and change, which can be reassuring to stakeholders who may rightly be skeptical in the aftermath of a problem. Winning over such stakeholders is more than half the battle in a rehab effort.

The best independent assessments take a "no sacred cows" approach and look to identify the root causes of a particular failure and assign accountability where appropriate. Law firms are usually tasked with these assignments, as they can preserve and assert privilege given the litigation that almost inevitably follows a crisis. Depending on the issue, other experts—such as forensic accounting firms, or specialists in cultural assessments or process engineering—can also be engaged to assist, most frequently working at the direction of the law firm to maintain privilege.

Issues around privilege and litigation are a critical factor in deciding how the conclusions arising from an investigation or assessment will be communicated. There are often good, legitimate reasons for not committing to provide every last detail around a situation. Discussing this dynamic early on in a rehab effort and agreeing on first principles before commissioning a review is always a worthy endeavor.

Changing the Narrative

On a corporate, organizational, or personal level, there is always a "narrative." Narratives—or stories—are always what the observer sees and believes they understand about a situation. Often in a crisis, even when a narrative is largely accurate, someone will say, "we need to change the narrative." This is, unfortunately, a code phrase for "we have a communications problem" and among knowledgeable crisis managers often elicits some eye-rolling. The fact is, changing a narrative—a cornerstone of reputation—is hard.

Narratives are an amalgam of impressions created by what people read about you, what they hear from friends and associates, and what they think they know about you. A narrative is your story and—for better or worse—a narrative is often a pretty accurate summary of who you are.

Of course, detractors who are aggrieved, who have an axe to grind, who are trying to gain some competitive, economic, or political advantage, or who are shorting your stock will sometimes push false or damning narratives so as to advance their own interests. Reporters with an incentive to shorthand controversy and complicated situations—and to generate stories that titillate readers—tend to be willing accomplices for such detractors.

But often, narratives are based on real things. Real reputation rehab and changing a narrative means understanding whether you have a problem of substance that needs rectifying. A good and brave communicator needs to push back when colleagues try to blame communications for a narrative, when bad facts are the true culprit. Too often, people look to ways to "spin" a new narrative without foundation.

Once you fully understand the narrative others believe, you can decide what you want to change about it. Put another way, if point A is the existing narrative, what do you need to do and say to get to a desired point B narrative? This isn't usually accomplished with non-substantive spin. Organizations that have gone through crises are under a microscope. Investors, customers, regulators, and employees all want to see real change. Communicating that change becomes largely tactical at that point.

Narratives that stick after the fact are usually based on demonstrable failures, for example, "Management stifled dissent or only wanted to hear good news"; "Tone from the top was bad." And the old saw, "The board was asleep at the switch." Such narratives are often pretty much all anyone really remembers about a crisis long past.

Rejecting an existing narrative—or parts of one—needs to be done with facts and substance to prove it wrong or outdated. It can't be because you don't like it or feel it is unfair, with nothing to support that feeling but frustration or a sense of injustice.

Changing the narrative in such situations means taking and communicating concrete, substantive action—including sometimes up to and including changing out the team under which the crisis happened (Wells Fargo, Boeing, BP, McDonald's). Accountability is critical in changing a narrative. Removing senior people or leadership, or even revamping the board, is increasingly what key audiences want to see before they will trust you again and begin to adopt a "new" narrative.

Can Your Employees Help? Internal Reputation?

For most companies, there are no better ambassadors than employees. Communicating regularly with employees, reinforcing positive impressions where they exist, and committing to change where there are negative sentiments is critical. Company leadership needs to be visible, engaging in substantive ways, and listening to suggestions around crisis response. Going back to the concentric circles, if your employees don't understand the issues or believe you are taking the right steps, you will never change external opinion.

Understanding employee sentiment about leadership, leadership's response to a given situation, and the impact on how proud or not an employee is to be associated with an organization in crisis is critical to ensuring that your employees are able to be good ambassadors. If they are embarrassed to talk to their friends and family about where they work, you have a problem and must take steps to fix it. This can take effort and time, but it is always well worth the investment.

Online Reputation Rehab

Social media and search engine dynamics can have a major impact on reputation rehab and need to factor into your planning. In 2015, research by Moz, an industry-leading search engine optimization (SEO) software firm, showed that businesses could lose 20 percent or more of their potential customers based on a single negative article appearing on the first page of search results related to the company.[6] And given that people surfing the internet about you or your company tend to gravitate to the most negative material, the very act of them clicking on a negative headline activates algorithms that keep the negative material on the first page where everyone can see it. Anecdotal evidence since suggests that the impact of negative online articles has only increased over the last six years as more and more people "live" online.

The desire to "fix" these issues can sometimes lead executives and businesses to popular digital reputation services that promise to solve the symptom quickly. These services can be successful in producing short-term results, but sometimes at a significant cost, as the tactics employed can potentially further damage your reputation online.

The goal in online reputation repair is to generate enough new and compelling neutral and positive content that pushes the negative content to the second, third, or subsequent pages. This takes time and concerted effort.

Services promising quick results around removing or pushing content down are frequently accused of deceptive tactics to "fool" Google and other search engine algorithms. A 2019 *Wall Street Journal* article, "How the 1% Scrubs Its Image Online," chronicled such efforts on behalf of a prominent hedge fund executive and even US Secretary of Education Betsy DeVos, for whom press coverage highlighting that her brother is former Blackwater founder and CEO Erik Prince was deemed unhelpful.

Firms promising quick action often employ tactics such as posting links across multiple networks of irrelevant and automatically generated blogs and establishing "click farms" to alter the behavior of search listings based on sending inauthentic traffic to favorable websites to temporarily exposc that content more prominently in the eyes of a search engine. However, it is good to know and be wary of the fact that Google regularly identifies these tactics and others that attempt to manipulate data. This in extreme cases can lead to being removed entirely from search results.

The "quick fix" SEO reputation firms—which effectively play "cat and mouse" with the big search firms—justify their tactics with the argument that it levels the playing field with search engines that tend to draw from more negatively biased sites. This argument can certainly be persuasive in some urgent circumstances. And it is a sad fact that it is harder than ever in this digital age to ascertain which is a "legitimate" news outlet. When faced with a particularly egregious search result, short-termist SEO tactics may be tempting and certainly temporarily effective.

The better path for most organizations, however, is a thoughtful, long-term strategy around improving one's digital presence, ideally having already cultivated over a period of time a variety of "owned digital assets" (e.g., Twitter, Instagram, and LinkedIn). Such assets should be developed for the organization and for senior executives who can weigh in helpfully in a crisis.

As executives become more active online, they can play an essential role in resolving reputational issues by bringing their personal leadership to life on these platforms. Every organization, large and small, should have an active and "always on" thought leadership program to support their digital reputation. This includes active profiles on social media channels like LinkedIn—for the company and leadership—that are regularly updated with engaging content. While this won't offer the "quick fix" of removing one specific search result quickly, the result will be a more accurate and stable reputation that can stand strong over years, not days.

Consistently developing thoughtful content that accurately represents the organization's mission are essential first steps in any digital rehab effort. Content should be authentic and relevant and include topics such as philanthropy, innovation, thought leadership on a pertinent topic, speeches, personal blog posts, successful business initiatives, and more that individual leaders can also own online on behalf of the company. This improves search results over time and enables an organization to proactively reach new stakeholders to further reinforce the positive aspects of a company brand.

Every organization and individual leader should be regularly reviewing "owned" assets online—including LinkedIn, Instagram, and Twitter—so they are accurate and maximized to include everything from the technical aspects of how search engines index a company website profile to how the organization or individual appears in third-party databases like Crunchbase and Wikipedia.

Advertising and Open Letters

You can't advertise your way out of a major crisis. Reputations are built and repaired by what you actually do. While advertising or paid-for "open letters" can be a useful tactic in getting across an unfiltered message (going through the media means your message is often heavily filtered), it only works when people believe the message. Paid-for ads are usually received skeptically. And campaigns that don't address underlying issues are doomed to fail or, worse, they can spur additional attacks if the ads are seen as "missing the point."

Message testing and consideration around the messenger and timing is essential to ensure that any paid-for advertising is on point and not counterproductive, for example, by making more people aware of a problem, or making people think you are trying to "spin" your way out of a problem. Reputation rehab is most effective when you are focused on communicating concrete actions that seem appropriate to what happened. Restating and recommitting to values can be useful when combined with substantive efforts to show that you are holding yourself accountable for living up to them.

Philanthropy

Targeted philanthropy can be a useful tool—both for cultivating allies and underscoring commitment to social good. Employees expect it and so do many customers. They all want to feel good about the company they work for and buy from. Consistent efforts over time and a commitment to causes that matter to your constituencies can be extraordinarily helpful when—in a crisis—you need friends and allies.

Donations and philanthropy after the fact—and efforts to publicize the effort while in crisis or soon after—can be viewed skeptically. Sometimes it can be seen as "penance" for what happened, and sometimes it can be seen as a transparent effort to "buy off" your critics. That doesn't mean philanthropy post-crisis should not be considered. Every corporation should use philanthropy strategically to advance its corporate mission and to demonstrate that it "gives back" to the communities in which it operates. It is never too late to start. Just make sure you have considered how your most skeptical critics may view a donation and how—if done in a ham-handed way—it might backfire. Sometimes it makes sense to begin making donations quietly without an associated publicity effort. For example, Wells Fargo, still struggling with fallout and customer trust issues from an overly aggressive sales effort, which resulted in the opening of accounts without truly informed customer consent, quietly launched food banks, which distributed food to certain disadvantaged communities. This initiative was well received and began generating community goodwill and customer trust. The point? To be seen as a net contributor to the well-being of the community and to enable new and different types of conversations.

Long-term efforts can also be undertaken to try to address a problem you are accused of creating. For instance, in the aftermath of the opioid crisis, a number of companies accused of looking the other way as it became clear that people were abusing the drug began efforts to support treatment centers. Boeing initiated efforts to ensure that overseas pilots had access to better training. This is long-term smart—especially given the questions raised in the MAX crisis and the fact that the aviation industry needs many thousands of better-trained pilots and mechanics to meet projected future growth. This is particularly acute in countries where the infrastructure to support highly sophisticated aircraft is lacking. This kind of philanthropy doesn't get you off the hook, but it is the start of a long road back.

Culture

Increasingly, when things go wrong, people look to whether a cultural problem exists (see Chapter 3). They ask if the organization encouraged or discouraged employees to raise issues and concerns, and whether, once flagged, the organization takes appropriate action. Cultural assessments run by outside consultancies are a valuable tool in many rehab efforts, helping identify how organizations really operate, what kinds of behavioral norms or disfunctions may have contributed to a problem, and what changes might be necessary to avoid future problems.

Tone at the top is critical, and that means looking at senior management and the board first. Is the organization living up to the values it espouses? Is it holding everyone, regardless of seniority, accountable? There has been in recent years a distinct movement driven by investors and activists to insist on "for cause" terminations over transgressions that might once have been overlooked or brushed aside. Definitions of what constitutes "for cause" and what might lead to forfeiture of severance have become and are becoming broader, specifically because it is recognized that bad behavior undermines institutional reputations and failure to address such issues forthrightly undermines confidence in a culture.

Today, it is expected that a company or organization will move more quickly on bad behavior to make a point and—frankly—to get ahead of potential public accusations that a management team or board is operating by different standards. There should of course always be a level of integrity in this process. Today's "cancel culture" and a sometimes frightening readiness to throw people "under the bus" can backfire if not thought through. Actions deemed by stakeholders to be simply performative or a deliberate distraction from the real issues and properly placed accountability can undermine your efforts.

Complicating Rehab

Something to bear in mind as you think about a rehabilitation effort is whether or not there are people, organizations, or competitors that may have a vested interest in prolonging your crisis or leveraging it for their own gain. Plaintiff lawyers, union organizers, and employee activists are especially adept at identifying where and when you are most vulnerable and using the media to increase your pain.

For McDonald's, unions that have long sought to unionize restaurant workers and which have regularly challenged the company on governance issues worked hard to leverage the departure of CEO Steve Easterbrook for their own purposes. On the announcement that the board had discovered new information about Easterbrook's departure—while some criticism about the extent of the previous investigation in 2019 was justified—the unions were able to rally some media allies to take an especially negative slant on board actions, which had been praised by most investors and employees.

Having a 360-degree view of contrary interests and a strategy to manage the issues they may raise is vital to ensure that your rehab messaging isn't undermined or contradicted.

Using a Crisis to Become a Better Company

At its most basic, reputation rehabilitation is about taking the lessons learned from a crisis to become a better company. It is a chance to assess what happened and why, to step up and responsibly address what happened, and to assess whether the company or organization is truly living up to its values. An honest, hard look at these things—and concrete decisions around actions to address disconnects—will enable positive change.

When a crisis is in Category #3 or #4—that is, some unforeseen external event has disrupted your business—the same applies. How did this event impact us? Were we prepared, and what "cracks in our system" did the crisis reveal? How should we be thinking about risk management, mitigation, and business continuity? Can we be better prepared next time? Did how we react to a crisis show us to be thoughtful, responsible, compassionate, and responsive in a way that comports with our values?

Whatever happens to your organization, rehabilitation means making sure that you are seen to "own the problem and the fix."

Rehabilitation Takes Time and Patience

Rehabilitation takes time and patience. Obviously how much time and patience depends on the crisis and how much time it took to resolve the underlying issues. A litigation tail can also make it difficult to get out from under the glare of a critical spotlight.

For most companies, the rehabilitation phase after a serious crisis—done well—can set a course for continuous improvement over many years. It may mean serious internal change—new people, new management, new board members. Or support for new regulation. Even divestitures. The full range of options beyond communications Band-Aids should always be on the table until they are not.

Don't waste the opportunity when a crisis happens to consider a silver lining, which is the opportunity to become a smarter, stronger, and better-positioned company for the future.

· IV ·

Repeat

12

Did We Learn Anything? Assessment of Lessons Learned from Our Handling of the Crisis

Just as a root cause analysis (discussed in Chapter 10) undertaken follow-ing a crisis can be useful to *prevent* a recurrence of crises, a self-critical postmortem about the *handling* of that crisis can be useful for improving the management of the next crisis, regardless of type. The bottom-line questions to be paused over by boards and managements are "how did we do?," "what went well?," and "what might we do better the next time?" Those questions relate principally to execution, but might also be asked about preparedness and recovery. The answers, together with the root cause analysis, will be relevant to evaluating management performance.

As Diermeier has said, a crisis can provide a "teachable moment." He asserts that Arthur Andersen could have learned from being investigated and fined by the SEC in 2001 for its handling of Waste Management's audits. As reported in the press at the time, "within the SEC, the Arthur Andersen investigation became the centerpiece of the commission's ag-gressive campaign to demonstrate that conflicts of interest were caused by consulting and other nonauditing services that numerous auditing firms [then] offer[ed] audit clients."[1] Had it learned from that experience, in-cluding from how it handled that crisis, it might have prevented the de-mise of the firm over Enron.[2]

A board and management should give some thought to how to con-duct the postmortem in order to maximize the benefits to be received from that exercise. One approach might be to engage in a process similar to what is sometimes followed for a routine annual board evaluation. The best practice for such an evaluation is to have a third party interview key individuals, applying Chatham House rules (report what was said, but not who said it) and reporting out orally. This exercise might be supple-mented by surveys of stakeholders. In terms of timing, the considerations applicable to a root cause analysis are applicable here as well. The post-mortem should cover preparedness, execution, and recovery.

Preparedness. Some crises will, with the benefit of hindsight, reveal gaps in risk management of a more general nature than might be revealed in the root cause analysis. For example, in response to its $5.5 billion loss in the Archegos matter, Credit Suisse announced that it was creating a new function to address counterparty market risk.[3] The lessons learned may have more to do with mitigation than with prevention. Consider the food contamination hypothetical used to illustrate the "five whys" in Chapter 10. One of the lessons learned might be that the company did not carry the right amount of insurance or that the exclusions vitiated the coverage. Or, that the company really, really needed to do war games exercises.

Execution. A postmortem of the governance and organizational aspects of the handling of the crisis might lead the board to feel that it should have been more involved in decision-making, or at least more frequently updated and better informed, during the pendency of the crisis. A nominating committee might conclude that there should have been an addition to the board mid-crisis of someone with the skills and experience who could help the company address its crisis. The management team might offer its views about what the board did that helped or hindered its management of the crisis. The CEO might conclude that the team he or she assembled did not include all of the necessary disciplines, that some of the outside advisors did not have a sufficient understanding of the business, or that one or more members of the team made it difficult for the team to work together in a collaborative and cohesive manner. A self-aware CEO (or one receiving candid feedback from his or her team or board) might come to understand that, to do better the next time, he or she will need to modify his or her leadership style during crisis. Or, that he or she discouraged members of the team from bringing forward complete information (including bad news) or expressing opinions. Or, that he or she was excessively crediting the point of view of one of the team members for reasons that were not fully based on the merits of those views. Both the board and the CEO might conclude that not enough attention was devoted to the normal business of the company during the period of crisis.

Looking back over the management of the financial aspects of the crisis might lead to a conclusion that the steps taken to preserve liquidity either overshot or undershot what, with hindsight, was needed. Perhaps a more incremental approach would have been warranted. This aspect of the management of the crisis, as well as the legal aspects, might have benefited from having better outside advisors or additional types of advisors.

Because the communications aspects of crisis management are so important and so visible, there can be much to reflect on after the fact. Did we appropriately prioritize among our various audiences (remember the concentric circles in Chapter 7) and provide consistent messages? Were we sufficiently careful to warn our various audiences of the dynamic nature of the crisis? Did we sufficiently consider the impact of our communications on the regulators who were considering what actions to impose on us due to the crisis, in order to prepare them for possible future changes in what we might be communicating? Did we have the right spokesperson and did we adequately prepare and protect that person? Did we use the right media to communicate?

From an HR standpoint, did we do enough for those at Ground Zero? Were we sufficiently protective of our key employees who were getting calls from the competition? Did we do enough to address the impact of the crisis on morale and our culture?

Recovery. As we discuss in Part III, recovery is part of the management of any crisis and involves both a root cause analysis and reputational rehabilitation. There can be lessons learned from how each of those elements were handled, and those lessons should be considered in dealing with the next crisis.

With respect to a root cause analysis, at the right time in the post-crisis period, it would be a useful exercise to step back and reflect upon a number of specific issues:

- Are there ways to improve upon how the process by which the root cause analysis was conducted? For example, with hindsight did we assemble the right team—expertise, experience, and candor? Would we have benefited from using an outside consultant?
- Was the scope of the analysis broad-based enough to be useful in preventing a recurrence of more than just the specific crisis from which the company is recovering?
- Did we identify the right remedial steps and did we create a system to provide adequate follow-up over the recommended remedial steps? That is, are we making optimal use of the outcome of the analysis?

Reputational rehabilitation is largely, but not exclusively, a requirement for companies dealing with crises that are self-inflicted—that is, those in Categories #1 and #2. However, even crises in the other categories, where the company is the "victim," might require reputational rehabilitation if the company is viewed as too easily victimized and the pain of the crisis is shared by some of its stakeholders.

Assessing the effectiveness of steps that the company has taken to rehabilitate its reputation starts with understanding four dynamics. First, some companies go into a crisis in what might be called a "reputational deficit." For those companies, the goal is more than mere restoration of reputation; what is required is establishment of an improved reputation. Second, when the crisis involves multiple players in the same industry, steps taken by each in the name of rehabilitation (like other elements of managing that crisis) will be compared. Third, Corporate America (and capitalism, generally) is not warmly embraced by all parts of the population. Finally, reputational issues may differ, as among the company's different stakeholders.

Accordingly, at the right time in the post-crisis period, it would be useful to step back and reflect upon the following:

- Did the tone of our communications during the crisis enhance our reputation ("empathetic, transparent, sincere") or detract ("spin" or "legalistic")?
- When developing the actions we took to rehabilitate our reputation, did we adequately take into account the four dynamics described above? For example, if one of the actions was philanthropy, do we look cheap compared to what another party has done or compared to our own financial resources?
- If we were dealing with a self-inflicted crisis and the remedial actions identified through our root cause analysis gave us confidence that we can prevent (or mitigate the damage of) a recurrence, without overpromising, have we appropriately communicated that to the relevant stakeholders in order to restore our reputation?
- Because reputation is in the eye of the beholder, what are we hearing from the media (including social media) and others (including critics and regulators) about our post-crisis actions?
- Should we engage consultants to survey our post-crisis reputation with stakeholders, as a way of more objectively ascertaining the effectiveness of our actions in restoring reputation?

* * *

Apropos of the phrase "lessons learned," we asked a handful of CEOs and independent board members to tell us on a strictly confidential basis (i) what was the best thing they did in preparing for and/or handling a crisis at their company, and (ii) what, if anything, they wish they had done differently. Here is what they told us:

- A CEO who had to deal with a number of crises over a long and illustrious career had a couple of things to say about the role of apology in managing a crisis. First, he passed along some advice he heard a peer give to younger CEOs in their industry—"When you have to eat a turd, and you surely will, swallow it whole." He then shared his own simple and unequivocal version of an apology, one that he had used during a press conference in the middle of a crisis—"It is our fault and we will fix it."

- Another CEO acknowledged the inevitability of crises: "We know crises will occur, but we don't know when. We have to think like a ship captain—knowing we will likely face stormy seas at some point. We cannot just sail along when times are good." And he urged a cautious approach during the "hair on fire" stage: "You need to acknowledge problems and respond quickly in a crisis, but sometimes we've moved too quickly—before we had all the facts. This can cause damaging credibility issues, where we've had to backtrack and restate information. You have to move as fast as possible, but no faster. With regard to attacks, charges, complaints, etc., against our organization, it's human nature to rally around the colleagues we respect and the company we love, and to push back. Instead, we should flip that inclination. For example, when presented with an accusation, we should ask ourselves where the accuser might be right, instead of where they might be wrong."

- Another CEO spoke of the benefits of "war games" (as described in Chapter 2). He went on to say this about mid-crisis communications: "If I were to do it over again, I would have encouraged our lawyers to allow more latitude and spontaneity in the execution of our external communications. People can tell when statements are written by lawyers, and an overly legalistic response can backfire—it's important to have balance. Our responses to crises were technically correct and successful, but they might have been done better with a higher level of visible personal leadership. It was difficult to achieve the personal projection of James Burke, the CEO of Johnson & Johnson during the 1982 Tylenol tampering and deaths."

- A CEO who led his company through the effects of 9/11 also spoke of preparedness. "No one can predict the actual contours of a crisis, but it is important to imagine what might go wrong, to have conversations around these things at the highest levels, and to have a game plan for the expected and the unexpected. Our game plan included assessing our various constituencies and their needs in a variety of scenarios. Probably the most important thing for me, however, and advice I would give is to discuss in advance how senior leadership should behave in a crisis and what might be expected of them." And he had this to say about execution: "In a crisis, there are often significant pressures to act quickly, but it is often difficult to assess in the heat of the moment the longer-term implications of specific actions. The lesson is that when certain actions are proposed, you really need to stop and consider the post-event implications."

- The former dean of an elite professional school who has served on numerous for-profit and not-for-profit boards provided the following observations that are relevant to any category of crisis: "I have learned how invaluable it is not only to have a team of talented and devoted people, but also to have them work together for the good of the organization as a team, without ego or pride of authorship in good solutions. Values of integrity, honesty, fairness, and equity—expressed and manifest at the top—are key resources to draw upon when a crisis happens."

- Finally, there's this observation from a director of multiple public companies: "You never know how good a board is until there is a crisis." That remark, taken together with the notion of the inevitability of crises, suggests that when a nominating committee is considering candidates, it might include "ability to deal with a crisis" in its skills and experience matrix.

· V ·

Other Organizations

13

What's Different for Private Companies?

Ownership concentration, governance, and requirements for public disclosure are the principal differences between private companies and public companies. While much of what has been discussed thus far about crisis management in the public company context applies to the private company, these differences translate into some important differences in crisis management at private companies.

Risk Management. In thinking about private company preparedness via risk management, we began with the hypothesis that the absence of public company shareholders reduces the risk of litigation based on the fiduciary duty of oversight (as discussed in Chapter 2), and that a result of that *might* be that private companies are less attentive to risk management than their public company counterparts. We tested that hypothesis by reaching out to a small number of individuals with experience with private companies—either as business school professors, private equity (PE) investors, venture capital (VC) investors, or otherwise. Some of the individuals also have experience with public companies.

The results of this small survey were quite interesting and informative:

- First, we were urged to differentiate between private companies that have PE or VC backing and those that do not.
- Only one of the respondents was in basic agreement with the hypothesis—which is good to hear!
- To the extent that private companies of any kind are less focused on risk management, that was thought to be based upon smaller size (and the possible lower degree of sophistication) and/or a generally lower profile, which reduces the risk of litigation and regulatory interest.
- As far as PE/VC-backed firms were concerned, one person noted that the typically shorter investment horizon may cause less focus on risk management due to an expectation that risks may not come

to fruition during the period of ownership. Similarly, if management turnover is somewhat more frequent in PE/VC-backed firms (as some have suggested), that may lead to continuity challenges related to risk management.

- On the other hand, those who felt that PE/VC-backed firms *do* focus on risk management noted that they do so because of the responsibilities they have to their investors, who might not sue them but who may decline to make further investments with them if there is a preventable crisis at a portfolio company. They also noted that they will be quite attuned both to balance sheet risk and, due to the fact that private companies may have less "bench strength," to the risk of loss of key personnel.

Execution. To use the parlance of corporate governance, in private companies there is essentially no separation of ownership and control. Private companies in which the founder or his or her family are still actively involved will have owners as part of both management and the board. When there are outside sources of equity financing (either VC or PE), those owners will also have representatives on the board. VC and PE representatives on a private company board are widely believed to be more engaged than the typical independent director of a public company.

As a result, when the crisis does occur, the "who calls the shots" discussion may be either very short or non-existent. Indeed, board members who are owners (or who represent the owners) will likely demand to be part of the crisis management team. That sets up a dynamic where the views of those people may have inappropriately outsized influence in decision-making about the path forward. This is despite the fact that the person with the most money (or even the most money at stake) will not *necessarily* have the best ideas. And an outside advisor who was hired because of deep ties to such a person may not give advice uninfluenced by what they think that person wishes to hear.

Moreover, the directors and officers of the private company (especially founders) may feel much more emotionally involved in the outcome of the management of the crisis than might be the case for independent directors of a public company.

Addressing the financial aspects of the crisis can be easier in some ways and in other ways more difficult for a private company. When the owners are "in the room" and represent well-heeled VC or PE firms, they may be a ready source of liquidity and/or have helpful influence in negotiations with outside funding sources. If a VC/PE firm has, shortly before the crisis, received a substantial payment from the private company through a special dividend or recapitalization, it will be very focused on preserving the solvency of the company. If management comprises family members several generations down from the founder, and if the other family members have come to rely on dividends, there can be significant hesitation about cutting dividends to preserve cash. A founder who is still involved in the business may have great difficulty in agreeing to a layoff of employees or a bankruptcy filing. When the private company is part of a private equity portfolio, it likely got into that portfolio through a leveraged buyout, and there may be less financial cushion available to address the double whammy financial consequences of the crisis described in Chapter 5. When a crisis occurs at a time that the private company is on the cusp of another round of fundraising or an initial public offering, that transaction may have to be deferred, if it is not totally derailed. That can lead to an unanticipated scramble for funding.

One of the biggest differences, of course, relates to communications—or at least the mandatory element of communications resulting from disclosure obligations under the securities laws. A private company, by definition, has no equity registered under those laws. It probably has no registered debt securities, either. Nevertheless, it will have disclosure requirements to banks under credit agreements and will be well advised to communicate well with lenders to maximize their support and cooperation. This fact reduces, but does not eliminate, a good bit of the pressure on the communications function. If nothing else, the absence of a need to publish an MD&A reduces the self-fulfilling prophecy risk of communications described in Chapter 6.

Moreover, the absence of public shareholders will allow the team managing the crisis to do their work without being concerned about short sellers, activists, or unsolicited takeover offers.

Even though the team managing the crisis will not be worried about the reactions of public shareholders and securities analysts to the company's communications about the crisis, the private company team must nevertheless be as focused as their public company counterparts on the reactions of employees. That focus will influence the communications program, as well as compensation and other steps to be taken to preserve the human capital of the company. Any crisis creates a risk of the loss of talent, and if that happens the value and future success of the company that emerges following the crisis may be diminished.

Finally, there is always the chance that a settlement with plaintiffs or regulators, a root cause analysis, a postmortem about the handling of the crisis, or a need for a substantial cash infusion from a third party will lead to a change in management. When that is the case, the private company may be faced with the need to buy out all or part of the position held by a substantial shareholder—even a shareholder who is a founder.[1] Indeed, when the crisis at a consumer-facing company is triggered by words or actions of a controlling shareholder, the best solution may be a sale of the company.[2]

14

What's Different for Universities and Other Not-for-Profits?

Universities and other not-for-profits are different from public and private business entities in a number of ways that have an impact on crisis management. A major difference is in the types of issues that need to be anticipated in risk management. There are also significant differences in revenue and financing sources and governance. Because many of the corporate leaders who are in the target audience for this book serve on the boards of these organizations, we think it is important to delineate some of those differences.

Risk Management. These organizations have to deal with many of the same types of crises as are found in the for-profit sector. They are no less vulnerable than business organizations to financial mismanagement, accidents, and #MeToo events (among others). So, they should engage in risk management along the general lines of what is described in Chapter 2 and focus on culture, as described in Chapter 3.

But these organizations also seem to be more prone to unique types of crises which, in turn, demand somewhat specialized forms of risk management as part of preparedness. Put another way, they will have a different answer to the question "what are the kinds of crises that we should be preparing for?" We suggest that they focus on four in particular: sexual misconduct toward minors, tainted philanthropy, excessive compensation and perks, and reliance on government funding. For universities, we add others: the need for a special emphasis on cybersecurity because of the nature of the research enterprise, and risks associated with operating a police force or a big-time athletics program. And some universities must also consider geopolitical risk.

Consider the number of infamous crises at universities and not-for-profits that have involved **sexual misconduct** toward minors or others. Sometimes that misconduct was engaged in by generations of individuals and lasted for decades (e.g., the Catholic Church and the Boy Scouts of America). Other times the misconduct was by a single individual and lasted much too long, but not for decades. In addition to the reputational impact, the financial costs caused by even a single individual can be staggering—for example, Jerry Sandusky at Penn State ($237 million), Lawrence Nassar at Michigan State/USA Gymnastics ($500 million), and George Tyndall at the University of Southern California ($1.1 billion). All not-for-profits whose mission includes working with minors or young adults should take these as cautionary tales and engage in risk management designed, first, to protect those in their care by preventing the misconduct and, second, to mitigate the damage to the institution from any such crisis.

Preventative steps include careful selection and background checks of the individuals who will be in a position to deal with "clients" and appropriate monitoring of those interactions. Staff training is also important. While training is not likely to deter a pedophile, "bystander training" can alert others to the need to be attuned to warning signs and the absolute imperative of doing something in response to concerning behavior. Perhaps the most important steps to take to mitigate the impact on the institution of sexual misconduct are to have an effective hotline for both victims and observers of misconduct, to be aggressively diligent in responding to any allegations of misconduct, and to broadcast and apply a zero tolerance policy in dealing with credible allegations. As to this last point, it seems clear that the severity and outcomes of the crises at Penn State and Michigan State would have been very different for both the institutions and their leaders if action had been taken earlier in response to allegations. And, more importantly, it would have spared many young people from the psychological and other damage (often long-standing) resulting from their victimization.

A crisis can damage the reputation of an organization and cause philanthropy to dry up. But it is also the case that **tainted philanthropy** can cause a reputational crisis. Consider the acceptance by MIT's media lab of donations from Jeffrey Epstein. Not only were the donations accepted six years *after* he had pleaded guilty in 2008 to a charge involving sex with a minor, but the director of the lab was alleged to have concealed the lab's relationship with Epstein. Harvard University had its own brush with Epstein and addressed his "extensive reach" in the magazine for its alums. While it stopped accepting his financial contributions in 2008, he continued an active relationship with Harvard's Program for Evolutionary Dynamics through 2018.[1] Another recent example involves the University of Cincinnati. In 2006, it accepted a gift from, and named its baseball stadium for, Marge Schott, the former owner of the Cincinnati Reds. This was 13 years *after* she was banned from baseball for a year for racial and ethnic slurs and eight years *after* she was forced to sell the team following an ESPN interview in which she praised Adolf Hitler. It was not until the aftermath of the death of George Floyd that this state of affairs attracted attention, to the detriment of the university's reputation.[2]

Not all bad acting is as visible as that of Epstein and Schott. As a result, a well-run development office at a university or other not-for-profit will do background checks on donors—especially big donors being considered for "naming opportunities." Of course, in the typical situation, it requires no small amount of subtlety and sensitivity to ask for money and at the same time do due diligence to make sure the prospective donor is a worthy individual.

Then there is the problem of the donor who checks out at the time of the donation but who is discovered after the fact to have had issues or whose issues occur after the donation has been accepted (and perhaps lauded). Case in point: the Sackler family, whose name adorns buildings and programs at universities and museums all over the United States. Do those institutions return the funds, which were after all derived from opioid sales? Under the terms of the gift agreements, can the recipients remove the name "Sackler" but not return the funds?

A variant on tainted philanthropy is the tainted board member (who is frequently a source of philanthropy). There have been instances where a sitting board member of a not-for-profit has admitted to tax evasion[3] or has been indicted for some crime or has been too close for comfort with a convicted criminal. The question for both the individual and the not-for-profit is whether their continued service on the board would be detrimental to the institution to the point of creating a crisis for that institution. If a board member's issues have caused him or her to lose their day job, it is hard to see how they could appropriately remain on the board of the not-for-profit.

The form of crisis that seems to be most directly hardwired to philanthropy is **excessive compensation** of a not-for-profit's CEO. Even when the organization can boast success in the pursuit of its mission and a good ratio of program expense to administrative expense, CEO compensation that is out of the norm can give donors pause. If the compensation is too far out of the norm, it can even lead to IRS penalties under Section 4960 of the Internal Revenue Code. Both donors and the IRS will be made aware of the compensation levels of the CEO (and others) by means of disclosure on the organization's IRS Form 990. Donors who do not bother to get the 990s themselves can rely on reporting by groups such as Charity-Watch (which publishes a "Hall of Shame") and Charity Navigator (which publishes an annual compensation study). Leaders' compensation at levels that raise these issues can be the result of a misguided perspective on the part of board members (who are often well-compensated business executives) to the effect that the organization's CEO is "one of them."

Even when compensation is at an appropriate level, flashy perquisites can also raise issues with donors and legislators. Universities that own or lease private aircraft for their presidents (or football coaches!) can attract unwanted attention—especially when the aircraft is made available for personal travel.[4] And when government audits of research grants reveal the application of funds—intentionally or because of clerical error—for the support of a university president's personal lifestyle, there can be problems for the individual and the university.[5]

Separate and apart from board-granted compensation and perks, a not-for-profit can be plunged into crisis by embezzlement and other acts of fraud by its CEO. Perhaps the most infamous case involved William Aramony, the CEO of United Way of America. By all accounts, he did a phenomenal job building up that charity, but lived a lavish lifestyle paid for by the charity (flights on the Concorde) and spent the charity's funds on a young lover. He was convicted of conspiracy, fraud, and theft; contributions to United Way fell for some time.[6]

Another type of crisis can impact philanthropy and employee retention at a not-for-profit—one based on assertions that individuals in leadership have "gone off mission." A recent prominent example came as a spillover from the sexual harassment allegations against New York governor Andrew Cuomo. The leaders of two different civil rights organizations were mentioned in the New York attorney general's report as having consulted with the governor about possible responses to the allegations before his ultimate resignation. At one organization, the leader was fired (and contested the termination); at the other organization, two leaders simply resigned.

For a not-for-profit that is dependent upon **government funding**, one of the risks it should consider is the reliability of that funding. The Jane Addams Hull House Association is an interesting case in point. That organization was founded in 1889, provided invaluable services to Chicago's neighborhoods (including foster care, for which it received payments from the State of Illinois), but was liquidated in a bankruptcy in 2012. This was in part because of the organization's overreliance on funding from Illinois, which was encountering its own fiscal problems. When added to the organization's leverage and addition of non-core services, this led to the organization's demise.[7]

Research universities can have a special challenge when it comes to managing **cybersecurity** risk. Research institutions design their IT systems to maximize collaboration among a large group of colleagues in a particular discipline. The resulting enhanced internal access can create an enhanced risk of improper access by outsiders. Those universities that operate academic medical centers have the additional burden of making sure that their electronic medical records and other aspects of their IT operations are in compliance with the patient privacy requirements of the Health Insurance Portability and Accountability Act (HIPAA), both for clinical operations and for medical research.

Many universities must deal with one form or another of **geopolitical risk**. This is most obvious for elite schools that have established centers in China, given the tensions between that country and the United States, as well as those with centers in the Middle Eastern countries, given the unsettled circumstances there. But even schools that have facilities only in the United States may have a very significant percentage of international students, whose admission is not on a "need-blind" basis and who thus pay full tuition. Limitations on visas can create a form of financial stress. Governmental scrutiny of foreign research funding and requirements under export controls laws and regulations have aspects of **geopolitical** risk that should be attended to.

Urban universities often have another type of risk to manage, especially if they are located in or near a high-crime neighborhood and operate a **police force**. Even before the George Floyd tragedy, these kinds of institutions recognized that an actual or perceived overreaction by one of their police officers when dealing with a member of the surrounding community could result in a substantial backlash. A well-run university of this type will focus heavily on training and background checks of its officers and on community outreach. It will elevate oversight of its police force to senior management and the board.

Universities with big-time **athletics programs** will need to manage the risks of a potential corruption of the admissions process (e.g., the 2019 bribery scandal uncovered in Operation Varsity Blues). There is also a potential for academic fraud. The University of North Carolina had to deal with a multiyear investigation (including the indictment [later dropped] of a faculty member) relating to allegations that athletes were taking no-show classes and having papers written for them. It was alleged that these actions took place over a two-decade period. While described as "one of the worst academic scandals in the history of college sports," and causing the university to be placed on probation for a year by its academic accrediting body, the NCAA ultimately ruled not to take action against UNC athletics.[8]

Finally (and perhaps most regrettably), there is a potential for serious off-the-field misconduct by individual athletes. When that happens, there must be a response; a failure to respond can seriously damage the reputation of the university and its administration. Take the case of the Baylor football team. After a football player was convicted of rape, its board hired an outside law firm to conduct a broad-based investigation. The 2016 report of the investigation included findings that "Actions by University administrators directly discouraged some [sexual assault] complainants from reporting or participating in student conduct processes and in one instance constituted retaliation for reporting sexual assault." These and other actions were said to "reflect a fundamental failure by Baylor to implement Title IX of the Education Amendments Act of 1972 . . . and the Violence Against Women Reauthorization Act of 1994." The recitation of the failures published by the Board of Regents included statements that read like a pathology report of poor risk management, which led to the crisis—"The football program failed to identify and maintain control over known risks . . . leadership . . . did not set the [proper] tone." Personnel actions included a demotion of the president. Although there was no assertion that he had direct knowledge of the actions of the players or other administrators, he was promptly "transitioned to chancellor"; he resigned from the chancellor position days later and from his professorial chair at the Baylor law school a few weeks after that. In a denouement five years later, the NCAA (on August 11, 2021) issued its "Public Infractions Decision" and concluded that it would not penalize Baylor, in part because "the football program's failure to report incidents . . . [did not constitute] impermissible benefits to student-athletes when there was a campus-wide culture of non-reporting." This finding (and the inventories of sexual assaults and various related actions against the university included in the decision) could revive attention to the case and, arguably, further damage the reputation of the university.[9]

Revenue, Financing Sources, and Financial Outcome. Universities and some not-for-profits derive some of their revenues from the provision of services. In the case of universities, that would be tuition and fees for room and board. But often a more important source of funding is from philanthropy. These sources can be adversely impacted by reputational issues associated with crises—especially crises resulting from the unique risk issues identified above.

When philanthropy has allowed a not-for-profit to build an endowment, a portion of those funds might be available to provide liquidity in a time of crisis—but, importantly, only a portion if and to the extent that funds have been restricted by the donor for certain purposes.

Another source of funding for not-for-profits can be governmental support—either grants or payment for services. In addition to the issue of reliability (already mentioned), that support, too, can be adversely impacted by crisis-related reputational issues, especially if that support can be affected by the views of elected officials.

Universities, like private companies, do not issue equity securities registered under the securities laws. They do, however, frequently issue bonds—technically, they stand behind debt issuances of state finance authorities. When universities engage in this form of financing, they have disclosure obligations and must deal with rating agencies. While the disclosure obligations do not have the same degree of intensity as what public companies must deal with, those obligations are relevant to the communications aspects of managing any crisis. And ratings of, and required interest rate on, such bonds can be affected by crises.

In an extreme case, the impact of a crisis on revenues and availability of financing can lead a not-for-profit to file bankruptcy, just like any for-profit organization.[10]

Governance. The governance of universities and other not-for-profits is different than what is found in public companies. Not-for-profit governing bodies tend to be very large, leading to a risk of "social loafing"— sociologists' term for "I don't need to pay attention, because someone else must be doing that." Legal disciplining of management and the board is typically in the hands of states' attorneys general, but that is rarely exercised. Moreover, state statutes typically protect directors and trustees against financial liability, other than in the most outrageous situations. As a result, unless there is a very attentive and diligent audit committee, there can often be a degree of casualness when it comes to risk management. When risk matures into crisis, however, the board members of these kinds of institutions can become very attentive, in an effort to protect their reputations, as well as the reputation of the institution.

· VI ·
The COVID-19 Pandemic

15

Observations on Public Company Responses

Throughout the year 2020 and continuing into 2022, both the public and the private sectors in the United States were grappling with multiple crises. Here, we offer our observations on public company responses to the Pandemic.

The Pandemic involved two interrelated crises—public health and economic. For governmental leaders, managing those dual crises involved a difficult balancing act. Prioritizing public health (through "shutdowns" and other restrictions) exacerbated the economic crisis. Prioritizing the economy (by relaxing public health restrictions) may have exacerbated the public health crisis.

Using the taxonomy of crises set forth in Chapter 1, the Pandemic falls into Category #4 (disaster affecting the core business). Unlike the government, our public company CEOs were managing the impact of the Pandemic's dual crises largely on a micro level. How did they do?

In terms of preparedness, for individual firms the Pandemic would best be categorized as a Rumsfeldian "unknown unknown," or even a "black swan." That is, while it is fair to criticize the federal government's lack of preparedness to address the Pandemic as a "known unknown," it is hard to fault individual companies for not anticipating either the Pandemic or the impact it would have on their individual companies.

From the standpoint of execution, the efforts of public companies will be assessed in the context of an interesting time in the history of capitalism in the United States. The Pandemic arrived at a time of significant attention to corporate social responsibility (CSR) and environmental, social, and governance (ESG) issues. At the investor level, this attention is reflected in the pronouncements of large institutional investors and the growth of CSR/ESG-focused investment vehicles. At the corporate level, this is symbolized by the Business Roundtable's (BRT) issuance in August 2019 of its Statement on the Purpose of the Corporation. (The current attention being given to CSR/ESG and the purpose of a corporation is significant, but not unprecedented. For example, during the Great Depression, a debate on this subject between Professors Merrick Dodd and A. A. Berle was published in the 1932 *Harvard Law Review*.)

In the BRT document, the signatory companies expressed "a fundamental commitment to all of our stakeholders," consisting of customers, employees, suppliers, and communities in addition to shareholders. The Statement was viewed by some as signaling a departure from the notion that companies were to be run with a single-minded goal of maximizing shareholder value. Put differently, the Statement was described as disavowing the position articulated 50 years earlier in the famous Milton Friedman *New York Times* essay entitled "The Social Responsibility of Business Is to Increase Its Profits." Others would not go that far, but rather viewed the statement as an endorsement of the notion that shareholder value can be maximized in the long term by addressing the needs of the non-shareholder stakeholders. Still others have criticized "stakeholder capitalism" as "virtue signaling" or labeled it "woke capitalism." Regardless of which interpretation you choose, the current attention to CSR/ESG provides greater latitude for addressing social issues to corporate CEOs and boards, but also subjects them to heightened expectations.

Some commentators suggested that the Pandemic would cause "stakeholder capitalism" to "suffer a blow" and that "many businesses put their corporate-responsibility programs on hold."[1] Another commentator noted that because of "the polarized [2020 presidential election] and its aftermath [some companies] may be tempted to back away from supporting hot-button social issues."[2] In light of those assertions, it is interesting to consider the performance of public companies in managing the crisis for the benefit of all of the stakeholders, especially employees and communities.

When it was clear that the Pandemic would plunge their companies into crisis, CEOs who were attuned to corporate governance concepts made sure they took steps necessary to make themselves the answer to the "who calls the shots" question of Chapter 4. This was best achieved by keeping their boards of directors well informed—in the early stages of the Pandemic, sometimes with weekly phone calls and Zoom meetings—and thus in a good position to fulfill their oversight role and to provide guidance and support.

For all of the stakeholders (including but certainly not limited to the shareholders), the most critical goal during the Pandemic was the survival of the enterprise—the "can we afford this" question of Chapter 5. With the exception of a few industry sectors, that meant dealing with a potential liquidity crisis caused by a massive loss of revenues in the face of significant fixed costs. Because the governmental response did not (and could not) fully address this issue for all companies, they had to reduce variable operating costs and address other uses of cash that could be deferred or eliminated. Companies cut or eliminated their dividends. They deferred or canceled capital expenditures and other contractual commitments—sometimes in reliance on *force majeure* provisions in contracts.

After a surprisingly strong economy in 2020 and the start of 2021, buoyed in part by the appearance that the Pandemic might be coming to an end, there was an expectation that corporations would once again be using cash for expansion and other purposes. At the end of the second quarter of 2021, cash and short-term investments on corporate balance sheets globally hit a record high of $6.84 trillion—45 percent higher than the five years pre-Pandemic.[3] These hopes about an end to the Pandemic were dampened (if not worsened) by the emergences of Delta and Omicron. In the second half of 2021, many companies reported "headwinds" caused by inflation, supply chain disruptions, and labor shortages.

The "can we afford this" question of Chapter 5 intersected with the "what about those lawyers" question of Chapter 6. Many companies sought recovery under business interruption policies. The potential claims under those policies were reported to be in the billions of dollars. Unfortunately for many companies, the insurance industry's "lesson learned" from the SARS experience of 2003 was to include "virus waivers" in their policies. Because of that, and other arguments available to insurers, many of the coverage litigation cases brought by insureds have been unsuccessful. Nevertheless, some insureds have argued that the losses were the result of government-ordered lockdowns, not the virus.[4]

The "can we afford this" question intersected with the "what about our people" question of Chapter 8. As a matter of survival, there were massive layoffs and furloughs of employees, resulting in record numbers of applicants for unemployment insurance. With an eye toward long-term shareholder value created by attending to needs of employees, however, significant percentages of large companies announced new or expanded sick leave for ongoing employees and continuing health insurance benefits for furloughed employees.[5] One company, Panera Bread Co., arranged for furloughed employees to fill open healthcare positions until they could get their old jobs back.[6] Executives and boards reduced their cash compensation, to preserve cash and (as importantly) to show a degree of solidarity with affected employees. This show of solidarity was somewhat tainted, in the eyes of some, because options were issued at a strike price reflecting dramatically (and often temporarily) reduced market values and, at some companies, the targets for cash bonuses were reduced. Moreover, cash compensation can represent a relatively small part of total compensation for senior executives. For example, in 2019 (the pre-Pandemic year), salaries represented less than 10 percent of the total compensation of the highest-paid CEOs at the largest US public companies and salaries plus cash bonuses were less than one-third of their total compensation.[7] Thus, a CEO who took a 50 percent reduction in salary might have had only a 3 percent or so reduction in total compensation. Principally because the stock market remained strong through 2020 (and beyond), a number of executives experienced significant compensation increases. This did not escape the notice of shareholders and proxy advisory firms, and in the 2021 proxy season "say-on-pay" votes went against a number of companies.

For employees who were not laid off or furloughed, companies facilitated work from home whenever possible. After working out the kinks in technology that facilitated working from home, CEOs pretty quickly learned that even those employees who had the "luxury" of working from home needed some extra attention. Some companies provided more time off for employees who were parents and had to combine work with assisting in remote learning. (In some cases, that resulted in backlash from other employees, and that had to be dealt with as well.)[8] Many CEOs learned that they needed to help employees address low morale and even depression as a result of a feeling of isolation or otherwise. They encouraged their managers to reach out to their team members simply to check in and to find "new ways to replicate how workers interacted in groups when they were in person."[9] They sought ways to have mentoring relationships continue remotely.

Companies that had extensive work-from-home or hybrid arrangements for their employees often recognized enhanced cyber risk resulting from less secure home networks and delays in implementing security patches. In response, they redoubled training and implemented additional security precautions.

When working from home was not possible, well-managed companies took steps to protect employees against the risk of infection, and some offered "combat pay." Amazon, which had been criticized for not taking sufficient steps to protect its employees, paid half a billion dollars in bonuses for those on the front lines.[10]

Careful planning was begun for how companies would reopen when the stay-at-home orders began to be lifted. That planning focused heavily on employee health, both out of a sincere concern for their well-being and also to limit litigation and reputational exposure. And one of the first actions taken by the new Biden administration was to direct OSHA to release guidance on employee protection from COVID-19.

Another issue for companies to grapple with in reopening was this: whether they would require getting vaccinated as a condition to returning to their premises. The legality of such a requirement was supported by guidance from the federal Equal Employment Opportunity Commission on May 28, 2021. And, if so, what would be the permitted exceptions? Should any such requirement be imposed during the period when the FDA had provided only Emergency Use Authorization for the vaccine? If not a requirement to be vaccinated, would there be encouragement (including by addressing anti-vax misinformation)? Would the CEO and other senior executives lead by example and take the vaccine?

In terms of mandatory vaccination for employees, the patient and cautious, yet ultimately successful, approach taken by United Continental Holdings (the parent of United Airlines) stands out as a positive example. Its approach to mandating vaccinations was described as involving "laying the groundwork . . . for at least a year" and "a gradual effort that started with providing incentives [extra pay and vacation days] and getting buy-in from employee groups, especially unions." This, despite being "part of a lonely group of large employers willing to broadly require vaccination."[11]

Really thoughtful corporate leadership took the issue of reopening a step further. Many CEOs understood that the post-Pandemic period was not going to be just like pre-Pandemic. That is, they realized that there would be a "new normal" that would have HR and other implications for how their companies would operate:

- Will employees continue to work from home at least some of the time? COVID-19 variants required employers to show some flexibility and, on occasion, backtrack on their "reopening plans."
- Will that create continuing opportunities for food and consumer products companies?
- What will be the future of open-office floor plans?
- Will retail customers continue to shop largely online?
- Will critical participants in the supply chain be there when they are needed and should there be greater reliance on domestic suppliers?
- Will women, who reportedly dropped out of the workforce because of the extra demands made upon them at home, return?
- How do we reinvigorate corporate culture after over a year of "working from home" and interaction solely via Zoom? And so on.

The answer to the "what do we say" question of Chapter 7 was particularly challenging, especially in the early stages of the Pandemic. For many companies, the unpredictability of the crisis (arguably exacerbated by the conflicting or ambiguous pronouncements from the government) meant that the best they could do was to withdraw earnings guidance.

The Pandemic also created opportunities for reputation building. For communities, companies that could afford to do so engaged in philanthropy. Others (under the threat of the Defense Production Act or otherwise) repurposed their manufacturing facilities for the production of personal protective equipment for healthcare and other workers on the front lines. Perhaps the most significant action for the benefit of communities (and a great example of putting people over profits) came when corporate CEOs urged caution on the timing of reopening the economy and insisted on testing as a condition precedent. For example, the Business Roundtable issued a letter to Vice President Mike Pence, as the leader of the coronavirus task force. In that letter, the BRT urged that in "developing economic recovery plans," both the federal and state governments should follow "overriding principles." The first such principle was "safety first," meaning "reopening at the right time, as guided by public health officials."

Not all companies fared well reputationally. Those companies belong in a rogues' gallery: large companies that took advantage of loopholes in the Coronavirus Aid, Relief, and Economic Security (CARES) Act and took financial support meant for small businesses; companies that lobbied to be included as "essential" when that would be a laughable designation; and companies that engaged in price gouging.

The response of the large pharmaceutical companies to the Pandemic has been very interesting. Those that were involved in the development of COVID vaccines read the early polls suggesting that a broad-based distrust of the Trump administration would cause citizens to resist being inoculated once a vaccine was made available. The response of nine of the leading companies was to pledge not to even seek FDA approval until proper testing protocols had been completed and established efficacy and safety.

In Chapter 1, we set forth a taxonomy of four categories of crisis and illustrated Category #4 with two examples—9/11 and the Pandemic. Interestingly, a CEO recently noted that lessons learned from the first of those crises informed how he responded to the second. In an interview in the *Wall Street Journal* about how airlines would ultimately come out of the Pandemic, Doug Parker, the CEO of American Airlines, was quoted as follows: "I did find myself harkening back to the 9/11 experience. I think that gave me as much confidence as anything—I know we are going to get through this. What's going to matter when this passes is how we treated our team, how we treated our customers. I think there are some people who are built for [dealing with severe crises] and some people aren't."[12] These quotations capture in a few sentences some of what we have tried to convey in our earlier chapters about learning from the lessons of a previous crisis, the importance of confident leadership, how attention to the "other constituencies" can benefit shareholders, and why corporate leaders sometimes leave at the onset of a crisis.

So, net-net, how did our public companies do in executing crisis management in response to the Pandemic? The answer to that question certainly varies by industry and even by company. Nevertheless, we believe that when the economic history of the Pandemic is written, US public companies—by and large—will be viewed as having handled rather well the most significant black swan event of our lifetimes. (And keep in mind that a number of companies were, simultaneously, grappling with "normal" crises unrelated to the Pandemic.)

Whether as a matter of survival or of corporate social responsibility (or both), the directors and officers of those companies stepped up to the task, benefiting their shareholders and other stakeholders. Indeed, there were times that many of those companies took actions that were needed to supplement the efforts of various governmental entities. Let's hope the leaderships of those companies (and their successors) will not have the "opportunity" to apply lessons learned during the Pandemic anytime soon.

· VII ·
Conclusion

16

What Questions Should
We Be Asking?

In the Introduction, we promised to focus on what questions to ask—questions designed to help prepare for, to manage most effectively, and to be in a position to recover and learn from a crisis and how it was handled. To fulfill that promise, and to provide something of a summary of the perspectives we have shared in the preceding 15 chapters, we are concluding this book with a list of questions. Most questions are appropriate for both a CEO and his or her board to ask, but (as you will see) some of the questions may be for one or the other.

- What are the highest probability risks that our company faces and that have the potential for putting our company in crisis? What is our risk profile?
  - Based upon our own history.
  - Based upon our new initiatives and challenges.
  - Based upon changes in the world around us.
  - Based upon our observations of our peers and what they have had to deal with.
- In light of that assessment, are our Form 10-K risk factors, our press release forward-looking statements, and our MD&A trends and uncertainties disclosures complete and correct in all material respects?
- If our key risks have changed, why is that the case?
- Is our team charged with risk management sufficient (in quality and quantity) to get the job done?
- Does our corporate culture add to, or mitigate, risk? Do we have subcultures that are aligned with the overall enterprise on risk management?
- Are we doing appropriate things (on a cost-benefit analysis) to prevent those risks from turning into a crisis or to mitigate the effects of such a crisis?

- Should we be engaging in "war games" and financial stress testing?
- Would we be able to quickly assemble a crisis management team covering the right disciplines and be able to work collaboratively?
- Will our corporate organization, compensation design, and reputation management put us in a good position to prevent or deal with a crisis?
- Is our board as a whole or through a committee sufficiently engaged in oversight of risk, especially risk the management of which is "mission critical"? And do we have individuals on our board who have experience in dealing with crises?
- Are we prepared for emergency CEO succession and shareholder activism?

EXECUTION

- What category of crisis are we dealing with? Are we being perceived as victims or perpetrators?
- In light of the crisis we are dealing with, is our board appropriately involved in oversight and decision-making, and should the board as a whole be engaged or is a committee an appropriate approach? Should we add a new board member to assist?
- Does the management (or the CEO) have a clear, or possibly subtle, conflict of interest?
- Even if he or she has no conflict of interest, is the CEO up to the task—in the sense of being able to handle the stress, act as our principal communicator, lead the team and mediate between conflicting positions, and change his or her leadership style to fit the occasion? Are any limitations remediable through coaching?
- Do the CEO and the board have a clear path to obtaining all information that will be helpful to decision-making? Are information sources invited to deliver even bad news, and do they accept the sincerity of that invitation?
- Have we assembled the right team of internal and external resources, covering all of the appropriate disciplines?
- When we are considering what actions to take in responding to the crisis, are we attuned to longer-term consequences of those actions?
- Do we have a separate team in place to run the ordinary business of the company and are they appropriately incentivized?
- Will this crisis cause liquidity issues for us—because of the cost of addressing the crisis and/or because of constraints on the funding of normal operations? If so, what can we do about it? What must we disclose in our SEC filings and/or reflect in our financial statements? Are we appropriately candid with our outside auditors?

- Should we be notifying insurers (property/casualty, business interruption, directors and officers, or other)?
- What litigation and/or regulatory actions against the company and D&Os should we be anticipating? Should our general counsel be issuing a document preservation notice?
- What litigation against others should we be pursuing (or preserving our right to pursue)?
- Are we sufficiently attuned to the fact that our crisis might also be a crisis for our regulators? If so, how do we keep their crisis from exacerbating ours?
- Do we need to worry about an unsolicited takeover proposal or an attack by a shareholder activist? If so, what should we be doing in anticipation? For example, do we have the right team of advisors assembled?
- Who should be our principal spokesperson(s)? What media should we be using? Do we have a process in place for establishing consistency in our messaging to various constituents? Are we being careful enough to flag the facts that any crisis is dynamic and that any statements we issue are based upon our understanding of the facts at a point in time and may become out of date or, even, inaccurate?
- Are we sufficiently focused on our own people as a target of communications?
- Are we doing enough (financially or otherwise) for preservation of morale and to avoid the loss of key personnel?
- Should we be financially rewarding those who are leading the crisis management team, and can that be done without triggering significant pushback from our various constituencies?
- Do we need to place anyone on leave? If so, with or without pay?
- Should anyone be terminated?
- Do we need to provide any of our people with counsel, either individual or "pool"?
- Are we, and our people, fully prepared for what might be a protracted period of stress because of litigation or otherwise?

RECOVER: ROOT CAUSE ANALYSIS

- Is this the time for a root cause analysis? Is it required as a legal, as well as a business, imperative?
- If so, what are the questions to ask to get to the root cause, and who should be asking them?
- Is the form of our RCA broad enough, or are we guilty of planning to fight the last war?
- What do we do with the analysis, once completed?

- When we decide on changes to make in light of the conclusions of the RCA, how will we make sure they are implemented and kept fresh and in place over time?

RECOVER: REPUTATION REHABILITATION

- Was there anything in our pre-crisis reputation that made it more difficult for us to manage the crisis? That is, do we need to do more than simply get back to where we were?
- What is the negative reputation that we have been burdened with as a result of the crisis?
- To rehabilitate (or perhaps improve upon) our reputation, do we need to do more than simply communicate that (i) we have determined and will eliminate the root cause of the crisis (see Chapter 10) and (ii) we have assessed our handling of the crisis and will address any shortcomings (see Chapter 12)? Will we also need to periodically communicate our progress in doing all of that?
- Would a failure to rehabilitate our reputation in the context of this specific crisis make it more difficult to manage a future crisis in a somewhat related area? For example, if we do not deal with the reputational hit we took in a #MeToo-based crisis, how would that affect our ability to address a crisis involving widespread sexual harassment at our production facilities?
- In whose eyes must we rehabilitate our reputation? If our biggest crisis-derived reputational issues are with our regulator and our customers, but we also have issues with our employees, will one size fit all?
- What is the full range of actions we might take to rehabilitate our reputation? For example, should we terminate or reassign any employees, add board members, establish a new standing committee of the board, support new regulation that applies to all in our industry, engage in philanthropy, etc.? Must those actions have a direct connection to the crisis we have dealt with, or might something less direct work or even be preferable? Can we reliably "test market" different approaches or is a leak resulting from that effort too great a risk?
- If other companies "shared" our crisis, what do we know about what they are doing by way of reputation rehabilitation?
- When should we begin to plan our actions? When should we execute on those plans—for example, should we defer some of the actions and use them in settling the litigation/regulatory proceedings that can take a long time to address (see Chapter 6), or would that dilute the perception of rehabilitation?

- What is the best way to communicate the actions we settle upon? And should they all be communicated at once, or put out over time?

REPEAT

- How did we do in executing on the management of the crisis?
- How did we do in our root cause analysis and reputational rehabilitation?
- Can we say that, from lessons learned (especially with regard to preparedness), we will do better next time?

Two final points about all of these questions. First of all, in the period of preparedness and the period of execution, they shouldn't be asked just once. Because things change and because crises evolve and cascade, they should be revisited periodically—during the period of preparedness, as often as semiannually. Second, as noted earlier, there is now a form of crisis that affects more than one company in an industry, either competitors or links in a supply chain. The answers to many of these questions will require an understanding, as much as possible, about what the other players are doing.

* * *

At one time or another, just about any organization will find itself plunged into crisis—whether internally generated or imposed upon it from the outside. The management of a crisis is especially complex for a public company.

Effective management can dramatically reduce the adverse commercial, financial, reputational, and human resources impacts of a crisis on a public company and, in an extreme case, can be the difference between surviving or not. Effective management will benefit all of a public company's constituencies—especially its shareholders and employees. Ineffective management can result in a change in management or changes in a board of directors.

The critical ingredients for effective management of a crisis are:

- Decisive leadership of a multidisciplinary team.
- Collaboration among the management and outside experts comprising that team.
- Appropriate oversight and engagement by a board of directors, including asking the questions set forth above.
- Careful communication, including selecting the right messenger, recognizing the need to focus most heavily on internal constituencies,

and realizing the need for consistency of messaging to the various constituencies.

- A recognition of the dynamic and evolving nature of any crisis, which may require changes (and even reversals) in both decision-making and communications.
- An understanding of the current environment in which any public company—especially one with a high profile—will be managing the crisis.
- Being attuned to the fact that a company's regulators may, themselves, be targeted for criticism because of the company's crisis.
- Studying the responses of the peer group when involved in a multi-company crisis.
- A corporate culture that, through words and actions, values and rewards risk-mitigating behavior, including candid internal communications.

Advance Preparation

Advance preparation includes multifaceted risk management. It also includes learning and remembering the root causes and lessons from the handling of any previous crisis. We stress advance preparation, because if a CEO and the board begin to think about crisis management only after the crisis has begun, that may be too late for an optimal outcome in managing that crisis.

For that reason, we hope this book is not placed on a shelf, behind glass, with a note reading "break glass in case of crisis." Rather, we hope that this book will be read in advance of a crisis and will help CEOs and boards of directors comprehensively and effectively manage any crisis that comes their way.

Acknowledgments

From Both of Us

While we each have separate groups of people to acknowledge, we want to jointly acknowledge a number of individuals and groups of people.

First, there are those clients who included us on their crisis management teams over the past decades. Whatever expertise and understanding we have (and are sharing in this book) is born of experience, and the clients were the ones who allowed us to gain that experience.

Then, we wish to acknowledge the CEOs and others who shared anonymously and confidentially their "lessons learned," as summarized at the end of Chapter 12.

Chuck Myers, our editor, and others at the University of Chicago Press run a process that helped make this a better book than we would have turned out all on our own. In particular, our discussions with Chuck beginning at the very outset of this project have been illuminating.

Finally, thanks to Tom's assistant, Cathy Chow, for her patient, prompt, and always accurate revisions of countless drafts of our manuscript.

From Tom Cole

I will start by acknowledging my co-author. In addition to collaborating with him on this book, we have worked together on multiple occasions as co-advisors to clients who were going through one form of crisis or another. Through all of those collaborations, I have learned a great deal and been able to serve the clients more effectively.

A number of others have provided a valuable contribution by reading and commenting on drafts of the manuscript. Colleagues at my law firm, Sidley Austin LLP, have provided important insights, especially through their reviews of Chapters 5, 6, 8, and 12. Those colleagues include Walter Carlson, David Gordon, Anny Huang, Dennis Twomey, Teresa Reuter, and Chris Abbinante. (I should add that the views expressed in this book are not necessarily those of my colleagues or our firm, and that any discussion of legal matters is current only through late 2021 and does not establish an attorney-client relationship between the reader and either Sidley or me.) Other reviewers who were especially helpful were Sam Scott (the retired CEO of Corn Products [now known as Ingredion] and a member of a number of public company boards), Carl Stern (the retired CEO of Boston Consulting Group), and John Rowe (the retired CEO of Exelon). Thanks also to Connie Cole, Alex Groden, and Emily Cole Groden for their substantive comments, editorial suggestions, and eagle-eyed proofreading.

Finally, as we note in the book in several places, crisis management can be a stressful endeavor. On occasion, the same can be said of a law practice. I am indebted to my wife, Connie, and our family for providing a welcome shelter from the stresses of law practice (and law firm management) for over 40 years. I dedicate this book to all of them.

From Paul Verbinnen

I will also start by acknowledging my co-author, who truly did most of the heavy lifting on this book, patiently awaiting my submissions and nudging when necessary. Tom and I have worked together on crises over at least 25 years and, as his many clients will attest, he is a rare talent. He has taught me much, and I am honored he chose me as his co-author.

I would also like to acknowledge my partners and colleagues at FGS Global, from whom I learn continuously. In particular, I'd like to thank George Sard, who co-founded our predecessor firm, Sard Verbinnen & Co. (SVC), with me, and also Peter Rose, a former client and vice chair of SVC, for their comments and insights on early drafts. My friend and former client, Martin Koffel, the former chairman and CEO of URS, also agreed to read the draft and offered many helpful suggestions—as did Niel Golightly, also a friend, former client, and now partner at FGS Global. Any faults in my logic or writing are not their fault—strictly mine.

Huge thanks to Olivia Bensimon, who worked with me on research over the past year, and my colleagues Scott Klampfer, Marc Minardo, and Scott Lindlaw for their valuable contributions to content.

Finally, I am grateful to my wife, Cecilia Greene, and my adult children, Andrew and Evy Verbinnen, who have always understood that crisis management can make a mess of the best-laid plans, and who have rarely taken me to task for it.

Appendix A
The Tylenol Murders

There's no question that Johnson & Johnson's handling of the Tylenol poisoning crisis of 1982, in which seven people were killed by tampered-with cyanide-laced capsules, is one of the best known and most frequently referenced crisis management case studies of all time. Applying the taxonomy of Chapter 1, it was a Category #3 crisis.

In the fall of 1982, seven Chicago-area residents died of cyanide poisoning after taking Tylenol capsules that had been tampered with. The first deaths were on September 29 and were reported the following morning in a medical examiner's press conference. Apparently, the first that Johnson & Johnson heard about the deaths came when a reporter called its PR department, asking for comment. On October 1, it was determined that the capsules had been opened up and contaminated. On the same day, J&J stopped manufacturing Tylenol in capsule form. A copycat case (strychnine, not cyanide) was reported in California on October 5. J&J asked stores to pull Tylenol off their shelves (a recall with a $100 million retail value) and, via the media, told consumers not to take Tylenol in any form—capsules or tablets. Within the first week, J&J had established a consumer hotline 800 number and another toll-free line for the news media to receive taped updates. Its CEO was highly visible—for example, on a *60 Minutes* broadcast. J&J also posted a $100,000 reward; the killer was never found.

Tylenol was a very important product for J&J—Tylenol reportedly provided 19 percent of its corporate profits in the first three quarters of 1982 and had a 37 percent market share for painkillers. J&J clearly put people before profits and succeeded in (correctly) being characterized as a victim. Moreover, it was able to recover. Through a combination of tamper-proof packaging and an aggressive marketing campaign, together with the consumer trust generated by its excellent crisis response, the Tylenol market share returned to almost pre-crisis levels within a year.

Of course, there was litigation. The first suit was filed on October 4. In 1986, J&J lost its insurance coverage case over the cost of the recall. And it settled with the families of the deceased in 1991 for an undisclosed amount. In a somewhat bizarre denouement, in 2011 a laid-off former employee published a book espousing a theory that the tampering took place at a J&J distribution facility. The company said the allegation was without merit.

Appendix B

Other Books About Crisis Communications

Lessons from Other Experts

There have been many good books written on the topic, and we want to acknowledge them. Some focus on case histories. Some offer "how-to" advice for management. And some are more academic in approach. While it is impossible to do justice to all of them, a reasonably comprehensive list can be found below, should you be interested in further reading.

In almost all of the books, big crises like BP's 2010 "Deepwater Horizon" accident in the Gulf of Mexico, the 2013 Target data breach, the 1982 Tylenol poisonings, the 2010 Toyota unintentional acceleration incidents, and many others are examined in fair detail. While these are broadly useful for any student of the craft, the key takeaway is that each crisis is different, and each has unique circumstances and politics that shape decisions, actions, and outcomes. Observations and critiques from the outside rarely capture critical nuances that are best understood in hindsight from those who lived through a specific crisis on the front lines.

As a result, none of the books get deeply into advising exactly what to say in a crisis because it's impossible to do so. It's always going to be situation and fact specific, but basic principles do apply—such as avoiding misleading or untrue statements, being clear about future actions and remediation, avoiding overly legalistic statements, demonstrating empathy as appropriate, and taking responsibility as required.

In his book *Chief Crisis Officer: Structure and Leadership for Effective Communications Response*, James F. Haggerty focuses on identifying a designated leader and team for managing a crisis, making the point that picking that leader and the right team isn't something that should be done in the heat of battle.

Haggerty outlines a process he calls "A.C.T.," which stands for "Assess, Create, and Train," as the best way to be prepared: "Assess potential crises and the teams will handle them; Create a plan of action that includes the checklists, templates, and other resources you will need in the event of a crisis; and, Train the crisis team as well as the broader team where applicable, and table top virtual scenarios to ensure the plan is executed properly in a variety of situations." The bottom line in selecting a team is to pick people with different functional and relevant operational expertise who can help you figure out what to say. Pick people with recognized good judgment, insight into the key facts, and a willingness to speak up and challenge assumptions. Cool heads are a must.

In 2011, New Mexico Gas was hit hard by a deep freeze across West Texas and New Mexico. Frozen pipeline valve and supply shortages meant that some 40,000 customers were impacted for several days. In what seemed like a panic move, the company promptly announced an ill-defined $1 million compensation fund as the crisis was unfolding. While this sounded good to the small team making the decision, there was no analysis to support that specific number. The knee-jerk fund announcement backfired, drawing several days of criticism for being insufficient and underscoring the fact that the overall operational response was, at least initially, chaotic. The better move would have been simply to reassure customers that efforts to solve the problem were underway, to triage those customers who were the worst hit, and to communicate that economic claims would be processed in due course.

The book *Effective Crisis Communication: Moving from Crisis to Opportunity*, by Robert R. Ulmer, Timothy L. Sellnow, and Matthew W. Seeger, makes the optimistic case that a crisis also represents opportunity, and that successful crisis communication "facilitates renewal." Put another way, while crises are to be avoided, they are inevitable. There is a way to get ahead of them, to learn from them, and to take concrete steps to prevent them from happening again.

The book encourages learning from failure and by looking to others and past situations to identify crisis risk in your own organization. In terms of what to say in a crisis, the book offers many solid pointers, including:

- Determining your goals: goals are often broad statements that can help guide decision-making and can connect to the larger values of an organization.
- Acknowledging uncertainty where it exists and reassuring constituents that you will maintain contact with them about current and future risk.
- Avoiding certain or absolute answers to the public and media until sufficient information is available.
- Avoiding categorical assertions and the impact a crisis will have on stakeholders.

- Giving practical advice on what people should do in response to a crisis.

In *Crisis Communications: The Definitive Guide to Managing the Message*, by Steven Fink, a key observation is on the difference between crisis management and crisis communication, an important distinction. Both are vital and, all too often in crises, the "managers" of the crisis aren't as aligned as they need to be with the "communicators."

Fink says in his book that both need to work together to facilitate the goal of matching reality and perception. While written long before Boeing's MAX crisis, this point was illustrated all too well in that scenario as the company attempted to reassure various constituencies about progress while serious questions about the assumptions behind that progress were being raised by pilots, regulators, whistleblowers, competitors, the media, regulators, and others. In particular, the discovery that Boeing knew more about issues with the software than it told pilots, and that it didn't move more aggressively to ground the plane after the first crash, served to dramatically undermine subsequent, more optimistic, communications.

Among some of the key lessons offered by Fink:

- "Always tell the truth. Time and time again history has demonstrated that it is not the act but the cover-up or the mountain of lies that brought down a leader or a company."
- "Telling the truth, taking responsibility, and letting your public know that you are on their side is not only a good price communication strategy but a good business strategy too."
- "Take control and determine early who is the right spokesperson for a crisis like yours. Remember it's your crisis, your message, and your spokesperson."
- "Even if you think you have everything under control, if the perception from the public is that you don't, they're right and you're wrong. Fix it."
- "A vigilant decision is one that is highly adaptive to the realities of the crisis; it is achieved by objectively collecting all available information, weighing the pros and cons, searching for either possible alternatives and most important actually making a decision."

The fast-moving and ever-changing world of social media is still one of the most challenging areas for crisis managers and communicators. In *Social Media and Crisis Communication*, an academically oriented book edited by Lucinda Austin and Yan Jin, the authors provide a variety of essays around how social media has become an integral channel for the message, and how failing to understand its influence can have a huge impact on your success. Many of the essays rely on W. Timothy Coombs's "Situational Crisis Communication Theory" (SCCT), which suggests sensibly enough that crisis managers should match their response with the level of threat the crisis poses to the organizations' reputations.

In the realm of social media and crises, most organizations are still working to keep up with how it really works, and this will no doubt evolve in the years ahead. Key lessons from experience are that:

- It is critical to really understand what is being said on various public and private channels, and to assess the true number of posts and the influence they have. Frequently, intense bursts of social media around an issue can lead people to think they are "losing the social media war." Good analysis and metrics tracking are vital to smart social media strategies.
- Fighting back against trolls who are not constrained by the truth, that is, posting corrections or challenging them, is tricky business. More often than not, it helps amplify their messages.
- Develop channels and build followings before a crisis, so that when one happens, you can reach important constituents with your message in real time.

Books to Read if You Want to Learn More About Crisis Communications

What Were They Thinking? Crisis Communication: The Good, the Bad, and the Totally Clueless, by Steve Adubato Jr. (Rutgers University Press, August 27, 2008).

Crisis Communications (PRCA Practice Guides), by Adrian Wheeler (Emerald Publishing Limited, 2018).

The Art of Crisis Leadership: Save Time, Money, Customers and Ultimately, Your Career, by Rob Weinhold (Apprentice House, 2016).

Strategic Communication in Crisis Management: Lessons from the Airline Industry, by Sally J. Ray (Praeger, 1999).

Crisis Management: Tales from the Frontline, by Caroline Sapriel (Crushed Lime Media, 2016).

Crisis Communications (Routledge Communication Series), by Kathleen Fearn-Banks (Routledge, 2016).

Effective Crisis Communication: Moving from Crisis to Opportunity, by Robert R. Ulmer, Timothy L. Sellnow, and Matthew W. Seeger (Sage, 2007).

Applied Crisis Communication and Crisis Management: Cases and Exercises, 1st ed., by W. Timothy Coombs, PhD (Sage, 2013).

Social Media and Crisis Communication, ed. Lucinda Austin and Yan Jin (Routledge, 2017).

Spin Sucks: Communication and Reputation Management in the Digital Age, by Gini Dietrich (Que Publishing, 2014).

Chief Crisis Officer: Structure and Leadership for Effective Communications Response, by James F. Haggerty (American Bar Association, 2017).

Leading Companies through Storms and Crises: Principles and Best Practices in Conflict Prevention, Crisis Management and Communication, by Yago de la Cierva (IESE, 2018).

Crisis Communications: The Definitive Guide to Managing the Message, by Steven Fink (McGraw-Hill Education, 2013).

Ongoing Crisis Communication: Planning, Managing, and Responding, by W. Timothy Coombs, PhD (Sage, 1999).

Crisis Communication: Practical PR Strategies for Reputation Management and Company Survival, by Peter Frans Anthonissen (Kogan Page, 2008).

Critical Moments: The New Mindset of Reputation Management, by Bill Coletti (Lioncrest Publishing, 2017).

Crisis Management: Planning for the Inevitable, by Steven Fink (American Management Association, 1986).

Crisis Communication: A Stakeholder Approach Hardcover, by Martin N. Ndlela (Palgrave Pivot, 2018).

Reputation Management: The Key to Successful Public Relations and Corporate Communication, 2nd ed., by John Doorley and Helio Fred Garcia (Routledge, 2006).

The Four Stages of Highly Effective Crisis Management: How to Manage the Media in the Digital Age, by Andrew Griffin (Kogan Page, 2014).

Damage Control: The Essential Lessons of Crisis Management, by Eric Dezenhall and John Weber (Penguin/Prospecta, 2007).

Managing Corporate Communications in the Age of Restructuring, Crisis, and Litigation: Revisiting Groupthink in the Boardroom, by David Silver (J. Ross Publishing, 2013).

Crisis Leadership Now: A Real-World Guide to Preparing for Threats, Disaster, Sabotage, and Scandal, by Laurence Barton, PhD (McGraw-Hill Education, 2008).

Crisis Tales: Five Rules for Coping with Crises in Business, Politics, and Life, by Lanny J. Davis (Threshold Editions/Simon & Schuster, 2014).

The Fixer: Secrets for Saving Your Reputation in the Age of Viral Media, by Michael Sitrick (Regnery, 2018).

Never Say Never, The Complete Executive Guide to Crisis Management, by Len Biegel (Brick Tower Press, 2007).

Lukaszewski on Crisis Communication: What Your CEO Needs to Know About Reputation Risk and Crisis Management, by James E. Lukaszewski (Rothstein Associates, 2013).

The Disasters You Should Have Seen Coming, and How to Prevent Them, by Max H. Bazerman and Michael D. Watkins (Harvard Business Review Press, 2004).

Notes

INTRODUCTION

1. Michael K. Lindell, "Disaster Studies," *Current Sociology Review* 61(5–6) (2013): 797.

2. Thomas A. Cole, "Business and Politics: When Should Companies Take a Public Position?," Harvard Law School Forum on Corporate Governance, May 6, 2021.

CHAPTER 1

1. Jennifer Latson, "How Poisoned Tylenol Became a Crisis-Management Teaching Model," *Time* (September 29, 2014).

2. Department of Defense Joint Course in Communication, "Case Study: The Johnson & Johnson Tylenol Crisis," August 21, 2019; Stephen A. Greyser, "Johnson & Johnson: The Tylenol Tragedy," Harvard Business School Case 583-043 (October 1982, rev. May 1992).

3. Rachel Louise Ensign and Ben Eisen, "Wells Fargo Ex-CEO Is Banned for Life," *Wall Street Journal*, January 24, 2020, A1.

4. Sally Yates, Deputy Attorney General, US Department of Justice, Memo "Individual Accountability for Corporate Wrongdoing," September 9, 2015; Rod J. Rosenstein, Deputy Attorney General, US Department of Justice, Remarks at American Conference Institute, November 29, 2018; John C. Coffee Jr., *Corporate Crime and Punishment: The Crisis of Underenforcement* (Berrett-Koehler, 2020).

5. Katherine Blunt and Russell Gold, "CEO of PG&E Steps Down Amid California Wildfire Crisis," *Wall Street Journal*, January 13, 2019, A1, https://www.wsj.com/articles/pg-e-ceo-geisha-williams-is-stepping-down-11547431270; Emily Flitter, Stacey Cowley, and David Enrich, "Wells Fargo CEO Timothy Sloan Abruptly Steps Down," *New York Times*, March 28, 2019, B1.

6. Walter Bogdanich and Michael Forsythe, "Rare Apology by McKinsey for OxyContin Work," *New York Times*, December 9, 2020, B3.

7. Vanessa Fuhrmans and Justin Scheck, "McKinsey's Leadership Vote Reveals Cracks in Its Global Partnership," *Wall Street Journal*, February 28, 2021.

CHAPTER 2

1. Daniel Diermeier, *Reputation Rules* (McGraw-Hill, 2011), 215; Richard J. Shinder, "The Age of the 'Unknown Unknowns,'" *Wall Street Journal*, September 17, 2020, A17, https://www.wsj.com/articles/the-age-of-the-unknown-unknowns-11600383351.

2. Frank H. Knight, *Risk, Uncertainty and Profit* (Martino Fine Books, 2014 reprint of 1921 edition), https://www.google.com/books/edition/Risk_Uncertainty_and_Profit/QxkKxhkl05sC?hl=en#v=snippet&q=measurable%20and%20unmeasurable%20uncertainty&f=false%20_.

3. Nassim Nicholas Taleb, *The Black Swan* (Random House, 2007).

4. Jonathan R. Macey and Joshua Mitts, "The Three Justifications for Piercing the Corporate Veil," Harvard Law School Forum on Corporate Governance, March 27, 2014.

5. Gillian Tett, *The Silo Effect: The Perils of Expertise and the Promise of Breaking Down Barriers* (Simon & Schuster, 2014).

6. Christina Ingersoll, Richard M. Locke, and Cate Reavis, "BP and the Deepwater Horizon Disaster of 2010," MIT (April 3, 2012), 4, available at mitsloan.mit.edu.

7. US Securities and Exchange Commission, "Proxy Disclosure Enhancements [final rule]," Rel. No. 34-61175, February 28, 2010.

8. *In re Caremark Int'l Inc. Deriv. Litig.*, 698 A.2d 959 (Del. Ch. 1996).

9. *Graham v. Allis-Chalmers Mfg. Co.*, 188 A.2d 125 (Del. 1963).

10. *Stone ex rel. S. Bancorporation v. Ritter*, 911 A.2d 362 (Del. 2006).

11. *Marchand v. Barnhill*, 212 A.3d 805 (Del. 2019).

12. *In re Clovis Oncology Inc. Deriv. Litig.* (Del. Ch. 2019).

13. *Hughes v. Hu* (Del. Ch. 2020).

14. *In re: The Boeing Company Derivative Litigation*, C.A. No. 2019-0907-MTZ, 2021 WL 4059934 (Del. Ch. Sept. 7, 2021).

15. Sidley Austin LLP, "Board Oversight in Light of COVID-19 and Recent Delaware Decisions," May 12, 2020.

16. *In re: Citigroup*, 964 A.2d 106 (Del. Ch. 2009).

17. F. William McNabb, "An Open Letter to Directors of Public Companies Worldwide," August 31, 2017.

18. US Sentencing Commission, "Guidelines Manual," Section 8B2.1(b)(2)(A).

19. Gary Klein, "Performing a Project Premortem," *Harvard Business Review* (September 2007), https://hbr.org/2007/09/performing-a-project-premortem.

20. Daniel Diermeier, *Reputation Rules* (McGraw-Hill, 2011).

21. Diermeier, *Reputation Rules*, 4.

22. Diermeier, *Reputation Rules*, 3.

23. Diermeier, *Reputation Rules*, 208.

24. Nir Kossovsky and Denise Williamee, "A Bad Reputation Is a Governance Risk," *Directors and Boards* (Third Quarter 2020): 30.

25. Luigi Guiso, Paola Sapienza, and Luigi Zingales, "The Value of Corporate Culture," Chicago Booth Initiative on Global Markets, Booth Working Paper No. 13-80, September 2013.

26. Jess Bravin, "Supreme Court Weighs Merit of Goldman Sachs Ethics Statements," *Wall Street Journal*, March 29, 2021 (reporting on case brought by Arkansas Teacher Retirement System).

27. Brad Smith, "Facial Recognition: It's Time for Action," December 6, 2018, available at blogs.microsoft.com.

28. BlackRock Investment Stewardship, "Engagement Priorities for 2020," March 2020.

CHAPTER 3

1. US Sentencing Commission, "Guidelines Manual," chapter 8, Part C (Section 8C2.5); *Marchand v. Barnhill*, 212 A.3d 805 (Del. 2019); National Association of Corporate Directors, "Report of the NACD Blue Ribbon Commission on Culture as a Corporate Asset," 2017.

2. Gary B. Gorton and Alexander Zentefils, "Corporate Culture as a Theory of the Firm," Harvard Law School Forum on Corporate Governance, August 3, 2020.

3. Edgar Schein, *Organizational Culture and Leadership*, 4th ed. (Jossey-Bass, 2010), 260.

CHAPTER 4

1. Ram Charam, Dennis Carey, and Michael Useem, "Boards That Lead," *Harvard Business Review Press* (2014): 222.

2. *Marchand v. Barnhill*, 212 A.3d 805 (Del. 2019).

3. Ben Eisen, "Wells Fargo Chairwoman Resigns Ahead of Hearing," *Wall Street Journal*, March 10, 2020, B1.

4. In re Puda Coal Stockholders Litig., C.A. No. 6476-CS (Del Ch. 2013) (Bench ruling).

5. Thomas A. Cole, *CEO Leadership* (University of Chicago Press, 2019), 44.

6. Cole, *CEO Leadership*, 48.

7. Erik Larson, *The Splendid and the Vile: A Saga of Churchill, Family, and Defiance During the Blitz* (Penguin Random House, 2020), 107.

8. Edgar Schein, *Organizational Culture and Leadership*, 4th ed. (Jossey-Bass, 2010), 244.

9. Daniel Golman, "Leadership That Gets Results," *Harvard Business Review* (March–April 2000): 82.

10. Natalie Kitroeff and David Gelles, "'It's More Than I Imagined': Boeing's New CEO Confronts Challenges," *New York Times*, March 5, 2020; Julie Johnson and Anders Melin, "Boeing's New CEO Regrets Blasting Predecessor as Backlash Grows," Bloomberg, March 7, 2020.

11. Roger McNamee, *Zucked* (Penguin Books, 2019), 152.

12. McNamee, *Zucked*, 160.

13. Cole, *CEO Leadership*, 64.

CHAPTER 5

1. US Securities and Exchange Commission, "Financial Reporting Manual—Topic 9, Section 9210," interpreting the requirements of Regulation S-K 303(a).

2. In re Carter and Johnson, SEC Rel. No. 34-17597 (1981).

3. ABA Model Rule 1.13.

4. SEC Rules 205.3.

5. AU-C Section 570, "The Auditor's Consideration of an Entity's Ability to Continue as a Going Concern."

6. US Securities and Exchange Commission, "Improper Influence on Conduct of Audits [final rule]," Rel. No. 34-47890, June 26, 2003.

7. Michael Liedtke, "PG&E Overhauls Its Board Again as Part of Bankruptcy Promise," AP, June 10, 2020.

CHAPTER 6

1. US Securities and Exchange Commission, Staff Accounting Bulletin No. 99—"Materiality," August 12, 1999.

2. *Malone v. Brincat*, 722 A.2d 5 (Del. 1998).

3. *Zapata Corp. v. Maldonado*, 430 A. 2d 779 (Del. 1981), 788–89.

4. In re Oracle Corp. Deriv. Litig., 824 A. 2d 917 (Del. Ch. 2003); *Martha Stewart Living Omnimedia, Inc., v. Stewart*, 845 A. 2d 1040 (Del. 2004).

5. David Enrich and Rachel Abrams, "McDonald's Sues Former CEO, Accusing Him of Lying and Fraud," *New York Times*, August 10, 2020, A1.

6. Sally Yates, Deputy Attorney General, US Department of Justice, Memo "Individual Accountability for Corporate Wrongdoing," September 9, 2015.

7. Rod J. Rosenstein, Deputy Attorney General, US Department of Justice, Remarks at American Conference Institute, November 29, 2018.

8. Brian A. Benczkowski, Assistant Attorney General, US Department of Justice, Memo "Selection of Monitors in Criminal Division Matters," October 11, 2018.

9. Lisa O. Monaco, Deputy Attorney General, US Department of Justice, Remarks at the American Bar Association's 36th National Institute on White Collar Crime, October 28, 2021.

10. Rachel Louise Ensign and Ben Eisen, "Wells Fargo Ex-CEO Is Banned for Life," *Wall Street Journal*, January 24, 2020.

11. Sarbanes-Oxley Act of 2002, Section 304.

12. Dodd-Frank Wall Street Reform and Consumer Protection Act, Section 954.

CHAPTER 7

1. Concentric circles have been discussed as an organizing principle in several texts dating back to Elmo Roper, a pioneering pollster, in 1945, who published a theory called "the concentric circle theory of public relations" to describe how messaging is transmitted to various constituencies. Many others have referenced or adapted the concentric circles as well, including Susan Silk and Barry Goodman ("Ring Theory" in *Psychology Today*) and Josh Kaplow in "The Concentric Circles of Crisis."

2. Target, "Target Confirms Unauthorized Access to Payment Card Data in U.S. Stores," *A Bullseye View*, December 19, 2013, https://corporate.target.com/press/releases/2013/12/target-confirms-unauthorized-access-to-payment-car.

3. Apple, "Update to Celebrity Photo Investigation," *Apple Newsroom*, September 2, 2014, https://www.apple.com/newsroom/2014/09/02Apple-Media-Advisory/.

4. Mark Zuckerberg, *Facebook*, March 21, 2018, https://www.facebook.com/zuck/posts/10104712037900071.

5. Sam Byford, "Samsung Recalls Galaxy Note 7 Worldwide Due to Exploding Battery Fears," *The Verge*, September 2, 2018, https://www.theverge.com/2016/9/2/12767670/samsung-galaxy-note-7-recall-fire-risk.

6. Johnson & Johnson, "Johnson & Johnson Issues Statement on Reuters Talc Article," *jnj.com*, December 18, 2018, https://www.jnj.com/our-company/johnson-johnson-issues-statement-on-reuters-talc-article.

7. "BP's CEO Tony Hayward (VIDEO): 'I'd Like My Life Back,'" *HuffPost*, June 1, 2010, https://www.huffpost.com/entry/bp-ceo-tony-hayward-video_n_595906.

8. "Blankfein Says He's Just Doing 'God's Work,'" November 9, 2009, available at dealbook.nytimes.com.

9. Boeing's Dennis Muilenburg, Boeing Chief Executive Officer, Q1 Earnings Call Q&A.

10. Natalie Kitroeff and David Gelles, "'It's More Than I Imagined': Boeing's New C.E.O. Confronts Its Challenges," *New York Times*, March 5, 2020, https://www.nytimes.com/2020/03/05/business/boeing-david-calhoun.html.

11. "Full Transcript: Ninth Democratic Debate in Las Vegas," *NBC News*, February 19, 2020, https://www.nbcnews.com/politics/2020-election/full-transcript-ninth-democratic-debate-las-vegas-n1139546.

12. Quote Investigator, "A Lie Can Travel Halfway Around the World While the Truth Is Putting On Its Shoes," *QuoteInvestigator.com*, July 13, 2017, https://quoteinvestigator.com/2014/07/13/truth/.

13. Erin McCann, "United's Apologies: A Timeline," *New York Times*, April 17, 2017, https://www.nytimes.com/2017/04/14/business/united-airlines-passenger -doctor.html.

CHAPTER 8

1. Stephen Morris, "Barclays Fined $15 Million by US Regulator over Whistle-blowing Scandal," *Financial Times*, December 18, 2018, https://www.ft.com/con tent/7625aa6a-02e9-11e9-99df-6183d3002ee1.

2. Edmund L. Andrews and Peter Baker, "Bonus Money at Troubled AIG Draws Heavy Criticism," *New York Times*, March 15, 2009, A1.

3. Craig Karmin, "Hyatt Executives Who Took Pay Cut Stand to Gain Through Latest Stock and Option Awards," *Wall Street Journal*, March 31, 2020, B1, https:// www.wsj.com/articles/hyatt-executives-who-took-pay-cut-stand-to-gain-through -latest-stock-and-option-awards-11585647000.

4. SEC Press Release 2015–54, "Companies Cannot Stifle Whistleblowers in Confidentiality Agreements," April 1, 2015.

CHAPTER 10

1. For example, search "root cause analysis" on Amazon.

2. "Guidance for Performing Root Cause Analysis (RCA) with Performance Im-provement Projects," available at cms.gov.

3. Ben Eisen, "Wells Fargo Shuffles Business Units," *Wall Street Journal*, Febru-ary 12, 2020, B12.

4. US Department of Justice, Policy Statement "9-47.000 Foreign Corrupt Prac-tices Act," Section 9-47.120.3.c.

5. Goldman Sachs, "Business Standards Committee Impact Report," May 2013, available at GoldmanSachs.com/BSCImpactReport.

CHAPTER 11

1. "Reputation Repair: The 5 Stages of Crisis Recovery," *International Associa-tion of Business Communicators (IABC)*, May 29, 2018, https://www.iabc.com/repu tation-repair-the-5-stages-of-crisis-recovery/.

2. Emily Stewart, "Two Black Men Were Arrested in a Philadelphia Starbucks for Doing Nothing," *Vox*, April 15, 2018, https://www.vox.com/identities/2018/4 /14/17238494/what-happened-at-starbucks-black-men-arrested-philadelphia.

3. David Taylor, CEO of P&G, "Safety Is No Laughing Matter," *Procter & Gamble*, January 21, 2018, https://us.pg.com/blogs/KeepingUsSafe/.

4. Capital One, "Information on the Capital One Cyber Incident," *Capital One*, September 23, 2019, https://www.capitalone.com/facts2019/.

5. David Yaffe-Bellany, "McDonald's Fires C.E.O. Steve Easterbrook After Relationship With Employee," *New York Times*, November 3, 2019, section A, https://www.nytimes.com/2019/11/03/business/mcdonalds-ceo-fired-steve-easterbrook.html.

6. Dan Hinckley, "New Data Reveal, 67% of Consumers Are Influenced by Online Reviews," Moz, September 2, 2015.

CHAPTER 12

1. Michael Schroeder, "SEC Fines Arthur Andersen $7 Million in Relation to Waste Management Audits," *Wall Street Journal*, June 20, 2001.

2. Daniel Diermeier, *Reputation Rules* (McGraw-Hill, 2011), 245.

3. Margot Patrick, "Credit Suisse Adds Risk Role to Prevent Another Archegos," *Wall Street Journal*, July 9, 2021.

CHAPTER 13

1. Anirban Sen, Jessica DiNapoli, and Jane Lanhee Lee, "Softbank Clinches WeWork Takeover Deal, Bailing Out Co-Founder," Reuters, October 24, 2019. However, that deal fell through a few months later and was recut a few months after that.

2. Katherine Rosman, "Greg Glassman, Embattled Owner of CrossFit, to Sell His Company," *New York Times*, June 24, 2020, https://www.nytimes.com/2020/06/24/style/crossfit-sold-greg-glassman.html.

CHAPTER 14

1. John S. Rosenberg, "Jeffrey Epstein's Extensive Reach," *Harvard Magazine*, July–August 2020, 27.

2. Matt Bonesteel, "University of Cincinnati Takes Marge Schott's Name Off Its Baseball Stadium," *Washington Post*, June 24, 2020, https://www.washingtonpost.com/sports/2020/06/24/university-cincinnati-takes-marge-schotts-name-off-its-baseball-stadium/.

3. Robin Pogrebin, "Carnegie Hall Stands by Its Chairman, Despite Tax Violations," *New York Times*, December 9, 2020, C1.

4. Greg Toppo, "Private Flights Rankle Lawmakers," *Inside Higher Ed*, March 5, 2019, https://www.insidehighered.com/news/2019/03/05/university-private-jets-may-be-practical-are-they-worth-optics; cbsnews.com, "Flying Coach: Many Universities Are Using Private Planes," February 20, 2017.

5. Jane Gross, "Stanford Chief Quits Amid Furor on Use of Federal Money," *New York Times*, July 30, 1991, A1.

6. Karen W. Arenson, "Ex–United Way Leader Gets 7 Years for Embezzlement," *New York Times*, June 23, 1995, A14.

7. Barbara Clemenson and R. D. Sellers, "Hull House: An Autopsy of Not-for-Profit Financial Accountability," *Journal of Accounting Education* (2013): 252–93.

8. Marc Tracy, "N.C.A.A: North Carolina Will Not Be Punished for Academic Scandal," *New York Times*, October 13, 2017.

9. Baylor University Board of Regents Findings of Fact, available at document cloud.org; Baylor University Press Release, May 26, 2016; Associate Press, "Ken Starr Leaves Baylor After Complaints It Mishandled Sex Assault Inquiry," *New York Times*, August 19, 2016; NCAA "Baylor University Public Infractions Decision," August 11, 2021, available at ncaaorg.s3.amazonaws.com.

10. Mike Baker, "Facing a Wave of Sex-Abuse Claims, Boy Scouts of America Files for Bankruptcy," *New York Times*, February 18, 2020, A1.

CHAPTER 15

1. John D. Stoll, "How's the CEO 'Stakeholder Pledge' Working Out? Depends Who You Ask," *Wall Street Journal*, August 28, 2020, B5, https://www.wsj.com/articles/hows-the-ceo-stakeholder-pledge-working-out-depends-who-you-ask-11598632678.

2. Dylan Tokar, "Will Political Polarization Stop Companies from Supporting Social Causes?," *Wall Street Journal*, November 20, 2020, https://www.wsj.com/articles/will-political-polarization-stop-companies-from-supporting-social-causes-11605868200.

3. Anna Hirtenstein, "Companies Are Hoarding Record Cash Amid Delta Fears," *Wall Street Journal*, August 16, 2021.

4. Jef Feeley and Katherine Chiglinsky, "Insurers Winning Most, But Not All, COVID-19 Business Interruption Lawsuits," *Insurance Journal*, November 30, 2020.

5. JUST Capital, "COVID-19 Corporate Response Tracker," as reported in *Directors and Boards* magazine Annual Report 2020, 9.

6. Francesca Fontana, "How Panera's CEO Learned to Go Against the Grain," *Wall Street Journal*, November 14, 2020, B5, https://www.wsj.com/articles/how-paneras-ceo-learned-to-go-against-the-grain-11605330030.

7. Dan Marcec, "Equilar 100," Equilar, April 20, 2021.

8. Daisuke Wakabayashi and Sheera Frenkel, "Parents Got More Time Off. Then the Backlash Started," *New York Times*, September 5, 2020, A1.

9. Katherine Dill, "What Bill Gates, Satya Nadella and Gen. Stanley McChrystal Say About Leading Through Uncertain Times," *Wall Street Journal*, October 6, 2020, B2, https://www.wsj.com/articles/what-executives-say-about-leading-through-uncertain-times-11602021318.

10. Dave Clark, "Amazon Recognizing Front-Line Employees with an Additional Special Bonus This Holiday Season," company blog post, November 26, 2020.

11. Niraj Chokshi and Noam Scheiber, "Inside United Airlines' Decision to Mandate Coronavirus Vaccines," *New York Times*, October 7, 2021.

12. Scott McCartney, "How CEOs Think the Covid Crisis Will Shape Flying," *Wall Street Journal*, July 14, 2021, A13, https://www.wsj.com/articles/how-ceos -think-the-covid-crisis-will-shape-flying-11626267600.

Index

About the Authors

THOMAS A. COLE is chair emeritus of the Executive Committee of Sidley Austin LLP. He joined the firm upon graduation from the University of Chicago Law School in 1975 and became a partner in 1981. He retired from the full-time practice of law at the end of 2016. As a partner, he served as vice president–law of Northwest Industries, Inc., from 1981 to 1985. For 15 years, ending in April 2013, he served as chair of the firm's Executive Committee, the committee that exercises general authority over the affairs of the firm. Throughout his tenure in firm leadership (and afterward), he maintained a robust practice on behalf of clients.

Mr. Cole focuses his practice on public company mergers and acquisitions and corporate governance. He is consistently recognized by Chambers USA and Chambers Global, including in their most recent editions. In 2001, Mr. Cole was recognized by Chambers Global as one of the 26 US lawyers included in its list of the "Global 100 Lawyers"—"lawyers who stand out from their colleagues and are recognized internationally." He was designated an M&A "Dealmaker of the Year" for 2007 by *The American Lawyer* and was selected for BTI Consulting's "Client Service All-Star" team in 2008, 2011, and 2014. In 2010 and 2013, he was named to "The Directorship 100," the NACD's list of "the most influential people in the boardroom community." In 2015, he was named an "M&A and Antitrust Trailblazer" by the *National Law Journal*.

Corporate governance assignments have included advising public company boards and their standing and special committees on a variety of subjects, including internal investigations, CEO succession, shareholder activism, and proxy contests. For the five years ending in 1998, and beginning again in 2013, he has taught the seminar on corporate governance at the University of Chicago Law School. Mr. Cole taught the same seminar at Harvard Law School during the spring semester of 2015. His book *CEO Leadership: Navigating the New Era in Corporate Governance* was released in November 2019 by the University of Chicago Press.

He has been involved in approximately 60 announced public company mergers, spin-offs, and takeover defenses, the majority of which involved values in excess of $1 billion.

Mr. Cole has been active in many civic, charitable, and professional organizations. He is currently a member of the Board of Trustees of the University of Chicago and chairs its Audit Committee. He served as chairman of the boards of Northwestern Memorial Healthcare and Hospital. He is a former co-chair of the Tulane Corporate Law Institute and former chair of Northwestern's Garrett Corporate and Securities Law Institute. In recognition of his initiatives in promoting diversity in the legal profession, he received the inaugural Thurgood Marshall Legacy Award in 2015. Mr. Cole and his wife, Constance, live in suburban Chicago and Kiawah Island, South Carolina. They have four daughters and eight grandchildren.

PAUL VERBINNEN is co-chair, North America, of FGS Global—and was co-CEO of Sard Verbinnen & Co. (SVC), which he co-founded in 1992 and merged with FGS Global in 2021.

He continues to be actively involved with many of the firm's clients, including public corporations, high-profile executives, and educational institutions. His former firm, SVC, was regularly ranked as a North American and global leader in M&A communications by *Mergermarket.* The company is also known for its work in helping companies prepare for activist engagement. Bloomberg has called SVC "Wall Street's Go-to Crisis Firm," and Chambers lists the firm as a Tier One leader in litigation support.

Mr. Verbinnen has worked on hundreds of M&A transactions and proxy contests, as well as a broad range of acute crisis situations, most of which his clients would prefer he not talk about. He also works with many companies and boards on corporate positioning, scenario planning, and preparedness. He also works with many universities and K–12 educational institutions.

Before co-founding SVC, he was executive vice president, international, for Ogilvy & Mather's public relations business, based in Hong Kong and London.

Mr. Verbinnen has a political science degree from Syracuse University and is a member of the Council on Foreign Relations and on the American Enterprise Institute's National Council. He lives in Florida and Rhode Island with his wife, Cecilia Greene, and has two adult children.